PRAISE FOR

What's Prison For?

"America's unjust system of mass incarceration tears families apart, costs taxpayers billions of dollars each year, and doesn't make our communities any safer. Bill Keller has been shining a light at our broken criminal justice system for years, and powerfully argues that America can and must do better. To do nothing or say nothing only reinforces the current nightmare. I hope you read this book, learn, and in some way, join the growing bipartisan efforts to bring about urgently needed change."

SENATOR CORY BOOKER

"A learned, lucid primer on the American prison system—its history and particularly on the best ideas for reforming it. Broadly sourced, intelligently curated, wisely explained."

TED CONOVER,
author of *Newjack: Guarding Sing Sing*

What's Prison For?
Punishment and Rehabilitation in the Age of Mass Incarceration

COLUMBIA GLOBAL REPORTS
NEW YORK

What's Prison For?
Punishment and Rehabilitation in the Age of Mass Incarceration

Bill Keller

ND
North Dakota SP

Oregon SP

OR

San Quentin

FCI Dublin

CA

Men's
Central Jail

Las Colinas

TX

CT

NY

Cheshire CI

York CI

Otisville CF

Bedford Hills CFW

PA

Sing Sing

Rikers Island

NY

• Attica

MCI-
Cedar Junction

MA

CT

PA

SCI Chester • Eastern SP

IN

Indiana WP •

LA

Huntsville
Unit

• Louisiana SP

© 2022 Jeffrey L. Ward

Published by Columbia Global Reports
91 Claremont Avenue, Suite 515
New York, NY 10027
globalreports.columbia.edu
facebook.com/columbiaglobalreports
@columbiaGR

Library of Congress Cataloging-in-Publication Data

Names: Keller, Bill, author.
Title: What's prison for? : punishment and rehabilitation in the age of
    mass incarceration / Bill Keller.
Description: New York, NY : Columbia Global Reports, [2022] |
    Includes bibliographical references.
Identifiers: LCCN 2022014399 (print) | LCCN 2022014400 (ebook) |
    ISBN 9781735913742 (paperback) | ISBN 9781735913759 (ebook)
Subjects: LCSH: Prisons. | Imprisonment. | Criminals--Rehabilitation.
Classification: LCC HV8665 .K45 2022 (print) | LCC HV8665 (ebook) |
    DDC 365--dc23/eng/20220513
LC record available at https://lccn.loc.gov/2022014399
LC ebook record available at https://lccn.loc.gov/2022014400

ISBN: 978-1-7359137-5-9 (ebook)
ISBN: 978-1-7359137-4-2 (paperback)

Book design by Strick&Williams
Map design by Jeffrey L. Ward
Author photograph by Emma Keller

Printed in the United States of America

"While society in the United States gives the example of the most extended liberty, the prisons of the same country offer the spectacle of the most complete despotism."
ALEXIS DE TOCQUEVILLE AND GUSTAVE DE BEAUMONT

On the Penitentiary System in the United States
and Its Application to France, 1833

CONTENTS

Introduction

In early 2014, I was invited to breakfast by Neil Barsky, a journalist turned investor turned philanthropist, who had an audacious proposition. At a time when news outlets were struggling to stay afloat, Neil planned to start a new one: a nonprofit newsroom focused on our broken criminal justice system. The Marshall Project, which he named for the civil rights giant and Supreme Court Justice Thurgood Marshall, would assemble an independent team of reporters and editors to investigate the causes and consequences of mass incarceration. To maximize its impact, it would share the work with other news organizations. He was looking for an editor in chief.

I'd spent thirty years at the *New York Times* as a correspondent, editor, and, most recently, op-ed columnist, but had never covered criminal justice, unless you count a few months long ago on the night cops beat for the *Oregonian*. So, before accepting Neil's offer, I did a little reporting, which marked the beginning of an education that continues to this day.

My crash course in criminal justice taught me that this
country imprisons people more copiously than almost any
other place on Earth. Some countries, notably including China
and North Korea, do not fully disclose their prison populations, so America may not actually hold the dubious distinc-
tion of first place. But there is ample justification for calling
what we do in America "mass incarceration." Our incarceration rate per 100,000 population, which includes adults
serving time in state and federal prisons and those awaiting
trial or doing short time in county jails, is roughly twice that
of Russia's and Iran's, four times that of Mexico's, five times
England's, six times Canada's, nine times Germany's, and sev-
enteen times Japan's. Our captive population is disproportionately Black and brown.

Much of the public debate was focused on the "mass" in
mass incarceration, a growing consensus that we lock up too
many people for too long. There was also considerable agree-
ment on how to reduce the incarcerated population—if we can
muster the political will. We can make some relatively minor
crimes—starting with low-level drug offenses—non-crimes.
We can divert people to mental health and addiction programs,
or probation or community service. We can abolish mandatory
minimum sentences and encourage prosecutors and judges to
apply the least severe punishment appropriate under the circumstances. We can raise the age at which accused youngsters
are subject to adult punishment. We can give compassionate
release to old and infirm inmates who are unlikely to pose a
danger. We can reduce the use of cash bail, which traps the poor
in the modern equivalent of debtors' prison.

14   In fact, the incarcerated population in this country has been in a gradual but steady decline since a peak in 2008—from 2.3 million to 1.8 million in 2020, according to data compiled by the Vera Institute of Justice. That includes an unprecedented 14 percent drop in 2020, attributed in part to early releases and locked-down courts during the coronavirus pandemic.

States have demonstrated that they can cut prison populations without jeopardizing safety. In the decade ending in 2017, thirty-four states, red and blue, simultaneously reduced incarceration and crime rates. Addressing the "mass" could also mean prisoners left behind would be less subject to overcrowding, which contributes to explosive violence and, as the 2020 plague year demonstrated, leaves prisons more vulnerable to rampant contagion.

This book examines the "incarceration" part of mass incarceration. Our prisons are not the most transparent institutions, and out of sight too often means out of mind. But the American way of incarceration is a shameful waste of lives and money, feeding a pathological cycle of poverty, community dysfunction, crime, and hopelessness. What is the alternative? Can we use our prisons to improve the chances that those caught in the criminal justice system emerge—and upward of 95 percent of them *will* emerge—with some hope of productive lives?

For more than two hundred years, there has been a tension between a punitive streak and a faith in rehabilitation, between treating prisoners as incorrigible Others to be incapacitated and shamed and, alternatively, viewing them as capable of restoration, even redemption. Opinions about how we should use

prisons have ranged from the mean-spirited "no-frills prison"
movement of the 1990s, which proposed to take away such
amenities as television and hot meals, to, at the other end of the
spectrum, calls for abolishing prisons altogether.

Assuming that outright abolition is not in our near future,
what kind of incarceration do we want for those we're not yet
ready to set free? What's prison for?

I begin the inquiry by recounting how that question has
bedeviled our politics over the decades, the historical context
for our current debate about mass incarceration. I continue with
a review of the research into how well incarceration accom-
plishes its ostensible purposes—punishment, incapacitation,
deterrence, and rehabilitation. The rest of the book examines attempts—some familiar, some experimental—to assure
that people return from prison better equipped than when they
arrived for the challenges life presents. It draws on what I learned
during my five years as editor of the Marshall Project, on the rich
reporting of my colleagues there, and on roughly a year of conversations with experts, advocates, and the men and women who
live and work behind bars. It is a work of journalism, not social
science or political advocacy, but I have searched both science
and politics for credible evidence of what works—meaning what
serves the legitimate cause of public safety while treating the
incarcerated as fellow human beings and future neighbors.

Like millions of Americans, I have family members who
have been victims of violent crime, including my wife, whose
mother was murdered in New York City in 1983. I understand
the yearning for retribution. But a humane society cannot be
driven solely by anger.

16 ## A Note on Language

Journalists, along with others who deal with issues of crime and punishment, have been rethinking the vocabulary we use to describe people enmeshed in the criminal justice system. As the Marshall Project's style guide puts it, the aim is to avoid stigmatizing individuals with labels that "narrowly—and permanently—define human beings by their crimes and punishments," and to do this without resorting to euphemism or bureaucratic jargon. I have tried to avoid labels like "convict," "felon," "offender," and "inmate" when referring to individuals. I sometimes use those problematic terms (as do prisoners themselves) when discussing *categories* of people. I also generally avoid referring to corrections officers as "guards," which many regard as diminishing their role. In no case have I changed language in quotations.

"Restoring Our Fellow Creatures to Virtue and Happiness"

On October 25, 1829, the warden of the new Eastern State Penitentiary, on the outskirts of Philadelphia, greeted his first prisoner. The log book identified him as "Charles Williams, Prisoner Number One. Burglar. Light Black Skin. Five feet seven inches tall. Foot: eleven inches. Scar on nose. Scar on Thigh. Broad Mouth. Black eyes. Farmer by trade. Can read. Theft included one twenty-dollar watch, one three-dollar gold seal, a gold key. Sentenced to two years confinement with labor." Whether he knew it or not, Charles Williams was a pioneer.

Eastern State was a Quaker-inspired project promoted by do-gooders (among them Benjamin Franklin) as a humane alternative to the traditional options for dealing with crime in the former colonies, which included public flogging, branding and the stocks, the pestilent squalor of local jails, forced labor, and, for even seemingly petty crimes, the gallows. The answer to crime, declared the Philadelphia Society for Alleviating the Miseries of Public Prisons, was not public shaming or corporal

18   punishment but "restoring our fellow creatures to virtue and happiness."

At Eastern State the cells had central heating and running water (amenities that had not yet reached President Andrew Jackson's White House). The lash was not employed, and the regimen stressed the reformative value of nearly complete isolation, prayer, contemplation, and busying the incarcerated with crafts like shoemaking and weaving. The concept had a fundamental flaw: prolonged solitary confinement can lead to severe mental torment, including suicidal depression. Charles Dickens, after a visit in 1842, wrote: "I am persuaded that those who designed this system . . . do not know what it is they are doing. . . . I hold the slow and daily tampering with the mysteries of the brain to be immeasurably worse than any torture of the body." But methods aside, the Philadelphia model established rehabilitation as a core mission of the modern American penal system. The very name—"penitentiary"—announced the guiding philosophy to be contrition and restoration, not merely retribution. Europe sent emissaries, including the French aristocrat and intellectual Alexis de Tocqueville, to study this novel American model of incarceration. (Tocqueville found the Philadelphia penitentiary regimen suffocating, rendering its subjects passive creatures, but he judged the concept morally superior to French prisons of the time, which made no attempt to reform their residents.)

Rehabilitation has been a mission often neglected in practice, especially in the American South, where prisons' main purpose after the Civil War was to provide a source of unpaid Black labor—slavery by another name. (The Thirteenth Amendment prohibits involuntary servitude "except as a punishment

for crime.") But the professed belief in second chances—in
"corrections"—has spawned a vast array of programs over the
decades: religious study, anger management, addiction counseling, parenting classes, trauma therapy, dance and theater
productions, TED talks, vocational training, and especially general education, from basic literacy to high school equivalency
classes to the pinnacle of self-improvement, college degrees. In
the name of rehabilitation, prisons have embraced everything
from the tranquility of Buddhist meditation in New Mexico to
the blood sport of inmate rodeos in Louisiana.

By 1972, this therapeutic role of prisons was so univer-
sally accepted that a US district court judge counted it "fashionable nowadays to say that only rehabilitation can justify
confinement."

Yet just a few years later another legal scholar would declare
the opposite, that "the conventional wisdom in criminology is
that rehabilitation has been found to be ineffective."

How the idea of restoring our fellow creatures to virtue and
happiness fell so precipitously out of favor was part of what the
Northwestern University historian Michael S. Sherry described
as a broader "punitive turn in American life." In response to
rising levels of violent crime, and to the movement for Black
empowerment, punishment supplanted rehabilitation in the
national discourse. The rhetoric and practice of crime-fighting
were militarized—the *war* on crime, the *war* on drugs. Sentences
became more draconian. In 1973, Carnegie Mellon criminologist
Alfred Blumstein, noting that the US incarceration rate had held
steady for half a century (except for a spike during the Great
Depression and a dip during World War II), had confidently
described a theory called "stability of punishment," speculating

20 that societies tend to settle on a fairly consistent level of retribution that makes most people comfortable. In late-seventies America, that stability came to an end. Prison populations began to soar from their half-century norm—roughly 110 of every 100,000 Americans—to 537 in 2021.

The proximate cause of burgeoning prison populations was a rash of laws fixing harsh sentences, and limiting the discretion of judges and parole boards. Legislators across the country enacted mandatory minimum sentences, three-strikes laws, and "truth in sentencing" policies that ruled out parole before most of the sentence (typically 85 percent) had been served.

Some of these measures had bipartisan support, albeit for contradictory reasons. Conservatives supporting fixed sentences complained that flexible—"indeterminate"—sentencing allowed lenient judges and parole boards to put dangerous criminals back on the streets. Liberals argued that this latitude let racist judges and parole officials indulge their prejudices.

The "War on Drugs" had no more outspoken champion than the liberal Massachusetts Democrat and House Speaker Thomas P. "Tip" O'Neill Jr. Reacting to the death from a crack cocaine overdose of Len Bias, a promising Boston Celtics draftee, O'Neill helped push through the 1986 Anti-Drug Abuse Act, which imposed mandatory sentences, asset forfeitures, and outlandishly severe sanctions on crack cocaine, which, unlike powder cocaine, was marketed in cheap doses to poor neighborhoods.

Being tough on crime meant being tough on criminals. Rehabilitation was denigrated on the right as coddling, while many on the left questioned whether any meaningful personal transformation could be accomplished in coercive environments like prisons, especially now that prisons were filled far beyond their capacity. As part of the Violent Crime Control and Law Enforcement Act of 1994, which then-Senate Judiciary Chairman Joe Biden shepherded (and President Biden later said he regrets), Congress not only financed a prison building boom and a militarized police force, it demonstrated its scorn for in-prison pedagogy by cutting off federal Pell grants for incarcerated college students. Most prisons that had college programs promptly shut them down.

Fearmongering politicians were abetted by some questionable scholarship and hyperbolic press. Political scientist John J. DiIulio Jr. conjured a myth of youthful "super-predators" that caught the media spotlight and branded a generation of young Black men as creatures without conscience. Sociologist Robert Martinson set out to debunk rehabilitation in a meta-analysis of prison betterment programs entitled "What Works? Questions and Answers About Prison Reform." (His answer: pretty much nothing worked.)

The hard-liners had their cheerleaders in the press, like the *Lowell Sun* editorial writer who declared in 1978 that the public "couldn't care less" about violence in prisons "as long as the murders are not committed outside of its walls. Let the bastards stew in their own juice."

The 1970s also saw the swelling of the victims' rights movement, which lobbied with great success for the voices of crime victims to be heard in sentencing and parole hearings. Understandably, these were rarely voices of mercy or forgiveness.

In the early 1980s, Corrections Corporation of America caught the punitive wave, pioneering the idea of privately run, for-profit prisons. The private prison industry, which is

22   typically paid the way hotels are paid, by occupancy, had little incentive to prepare prisoners for release. Shane Bauer, a *Mother Jones* investigative journalist who spent four months working undercover as a guard at a CCA prison in Louisiana, described how a "relentless focus on the bottom line" contributed to an atmosphere of cruelty and corruption. Bauer pointed out that profit has been a guiding motivation in penal practices since before the American Revolution, notably in the form of prisoners rented out to perform forced labor for private contractors. But it took the Reagan-era passion for privatization of government to bring out the full potential of correctional capitalism.

Private prisons now house about 7 percent of state prison inmates, and about 17 percent of the smaller federal system. The business has metastasized into a large, little-regulated, and often predatory industry of corrections services, feeding on contracts to supply transportation, telecommunications, clothing, mess halls, commissaries, medical care, halfway houses, and—a growing profit center in the Trump years—immigration detention centers. To the question, what is prison for, this industry introduced a new answer: shareholder value.

That's not the only sense in which prison inmates are commodities. For decades, towns in need of employers lobbied for new prisons, anticipating stable government jobs and a boon to local businesses. More recently some prison towns have become disenchanted as they realized that prisons don't necessarily buy their goods locally and that they make expensive demands on local courts. But the scattering of prisons as pork barrel projects created, in effect, company towns—often far from the families of the incarcerated, and from nonprofit support services.

Around the turn of the twenty-first century, rehabilitation seemed to be making a comeback. Crime rates plummeted and plateaued at the lowest level in decades. In 1994, the year that President Clinton signed that infamous crime bill, 37 percent of Americans identified crime as the nation's most important problem. By 2012, the number was 2 percent.

One thing raising hopes for a less punitive approach to crime was a political force few saw coming: a reform movement on the right.

In April 1993, Patrick J. Nolan was indicted on charges of racketeering, conspiracy, extortion, and money laundering. Nolan, an earnest law-and-order conservative, was the leader of the Republican minority in the California Assembly when he was caught up in an FBI sting. Facing the possibility he could be in prison until his young children were in their twenties, he quit his seat and admitted to one felony count of racketeering in exchange for a sentence of thirty-three months.

Prison reformers like to say that if a conservative is a liberal who has been mugged, a liberal is a conservative who has served time. Nolan did not emerge from prison appreciably less conservative, but he experienced a profound disillusionment, which led him to play a central role in a cause that, when I met him in 2015, was finding its moment: a rising conservative clamor to repair the criminal justice system.

Several candidates competing to be the Republican presidential nominee in 2016—Rand Paul, Jeb Bush, Rick Perry, and Ted Cruz—had been embraced by Right on Crime, a campaign to promote "successful, conservative solutions" to the punitive excesses of American law and order. The American

24   Conservative Union's annual Conservative Political Action
Conference, an event that serves as an audition for right-wing
presidential aspirants, featured three panels on criminal justice reform, including one called "Prosecutors Gone Wild." Ber-
nard Kerik, who was Rudolph Giuliani's police commissioner
and served three years in prison for tax fraud and other crimes,
was promoting an agenda of reforms, including voting rights for
ex-felons. The libertarian billionaires Charles and David Koch
were donating money to the National Association of Criminal
Defense Lawyers, to help insure that indigent defendants get
competent legal representation, and they were co-sponsoring
conferences on judicial reform with the American Civil Liber-
ties Union.

Pat Nolan had become the director of a new Center for Criminal Justice Reform at the American Conservative Union Foundation, tracking the progress of reforms state by state, drafting
op-eds for fellow conservatives, planning conferences, rallying
state legislators by phone, and firing off volleys on Twitter.

In Congress and the states, conservatives and liberals
began to find some common ground on such issues as cutting
back mandatory-minimum sentences; using probation, treatment, and community service as alternatives to prison for
low-level crimes; raising the age of juvenile-court jurisdictions; limiting solitary confinement; curtailing the practice of
confiscating assets; rewriting the rules of probation and parole
to avoid sending offenders back to prison on technicalities;
restoring education and job training in prisons; allowing prisoners time off for committing to rehabilitation; and easing the
reentry of those who have served time by expunging some criminal records and by lowering barriers to employment, education,

and housing. As David Dagan and Steven M. Teles wrote, in the
Annals of the American Academy of Political and Social Science,
"Retrenching the carceral state is becoming as orthodox on the
Right as building it was just a few short years ago." They con-
cluded that this had created a "Nixon goes to China" opportu-
nity to reverse decades of punitive overkill.

This conservative transformation was regarded with suspicion by some progressives as a ploy to cut taxes, shrink government, and turn prisons over to the private corrections
industry, and one of the motives was indeed a belief that downsizing prisons promised taxpayers a windfall. But for many conservatives, Nolan insists, reducing spending is "ancillary." "It's
human dignity that really motivates us."

"I went to the legislature very pro-cop and with a get-
tough-on-crime attitude," Nolan told me. The FBI sting, he says,
dispelled his unconditional faith in law enforcement. In Nolan's
telling of it, trophy-hunting agents browbeat his aides and his
campaign supporters to build a case against him, leaking tid-
bits to the press in the hope of breaking his resolve. The prosecutor loaded the charge sheet so heavily that Nolan concluded
that he couldn't risk going before a jury. Like roughly 95 percent of people convicted in America, he pleaded guilty and took
a lesser sentence rather than take his chances at trial. He began
to wonder how many of the people he had dismissed as bad guys
had simply succumbed to prosecutorial bullying.

By the standards of American incarceration, Nolan had
it easy. He served twenty-five months in prisons that housed
the least menacing residents. The Federal Prison Camp at
Dublin, near San Francisco, was a former Army barracks sur-
rounded by landscaped flower gardens. There was a small coterie

26   of white-collar criminals, but the majority of the inmates were Black and Latino men serving time for relatively minor drug convictions. Nolan helped organize religious-study groups, and—to judge by his accounts in an unpublished memoir—he treated his fellow inmates as a constituency to be charmed. (He still corresponds with some of them.) Still, his time in prison exposed him to what he came to see as the cynical cycle of American justice: sweep up young men, mostly from broken families in underprivileged neighborhoods, put them away for a while, send them back onto the streets with no skills, and repeat. To call this a "corrections" system seemed a sour joke.

"I had assumed they did all they could to help prepare the guys to return to society and make a better life," Nolan told me. "But they were just warehousing them." There was a pervasive sense of defeat. When prisoners were released, the guards would say, "See you in a few months." He was surprised, too, at the number of elderly and infirm inmates. In his memoir, he wrote that "incarcerating people who aren't a physical threat to society is expensive and counter-productive"—something that "only a nation that is rich and vindictive" would do.

"Above all, conservatives should ask themselves how likely it is that these bloated bureaucracies . . . will turn out to be any less rapacious, irresponsible, or concerned with the rights of ordinary Americans than, say, the IRS, just because they are packaged and marketed under the dishonest label 'tough on crime.'"

Paroled, Nolan was recruited by Charles Colson, a Nixon White House aide who had become a devout Evangelical Christian shortly before serving seven months in a federal prison for his part in the Watergate scandal. Colson had organized the

Prison Fellowship, a network of volunteers who visited inmates and promoted faith as a path back into society's good graces. Nolan was hired to launch a political offshoot, called the Justice Fellowship. The idea was to build a grassroots campaign to lobby Congress and state lawmakers for more humane treatment of inmates during and after incarceration.

After George W. Bush was reelected, in 2004, and the Republican majorities in Congress were strengthened, Nolan began hosting occasional off-the-record lunches where you might have seen libertarians from the Cato Institute, advocates of judicial restraint from the Federalist Society, social conservatives from the Family Research Council, and hard-core fiscal conservatives like the anti-tax lobbyist Grover Norquist. Attendees found a unifying theme in the arrogance and the overreach of government and the toll that it took on individual freedom and responsibility. Nolan became, mostly behind the scenes, a trusted broker, strategist, theoretician, fundraiser, diplomat, and whip. "If Pat says something, it's kind of the final word," Richard Viguerie, a far-right fundraising impresario, told me.

The most significant question is whether conservatives are prepared to face the cost of the remedies, from in-prison education, job training, and therapy to more robust drug and mental-health treatment as an alternative to prison. Joan Petersilia, a criminologist who taught at the Stanford Law School until her death in 2019, pointed to the previous great American exercise in decarceration, half a century ago: President Kennedy's Community Mental Health Act, which aimed to reduce by half the number of patients in state mental hospitals. The promised alternatives—hundreds of community care facilities—were never fully funded, and thousands of deeply

28   troubled people were liberated into homelessness. The mentally ill now make up a substantial portion of inmates in state prisons and county jails.

"The direction forward is not really clear, because, on the one hand, the right is saying less government, less spending," Petersilia told me. "And the left is saying we need more investment." She offers the example of California, which has been under a Supreme Court order to cull the overcrowded prisons that Pat Nolan, as a state legislator, once helped build. "The success story of downsizing prisons in California is like nothing the nation has ever experienced," she said. "We have downsized in less than five years 25 percent of all prison populations. But look what is happening at the local, community level, which is that they've upsized jails, and they've got a homeless population, they've got police officers complaining about the mentally ill. We didn't answer the question: If not prisons, what?"

Still, there seemed to be a tectonic shift in the culture. Prison reform became part of a broader campaign on the left to combat social injustice and a profound introspection about race. A new generation (my two daughters included) came of age in safer cities and seemed more alert to the inequities of the justice system.

The opioid crisis introduced many in white America to the realities of the criminal justice system, and raised uncomfortable questions about why drug use by people of color was treated as a crime problem while drug use by whites was a public health problem.

Then came conscience-pricking bestsellers like Michelle Alexander's *The New Jim Crow* and Bryan Stevenson's *Just Mercy*,

and then the horrifying viral videos of Black Americans dying
at the hands of white cops. There seemed to be real potential
for a new public consensus on the counterproductive cruelty of
America's answers to crime. President Biden voiced contrition
for the excesses of his 1994 crime bill, vowed to combat mandatory minimum sentences, and promised to "stop corporations
from profiteering from incarceration."

Even President Trump paid homage to rehabilitation,
signing into law the First Step Act of 2018, which allowed some
prisoners to shorten their sentences by participating in counseling and education programs. Trump's claim to be a champion
of reform was undermined by his racist law-and-order rhetoric,
his enthusiasm for the death penalty, and his predilection for
pardoning political cronies while ignoring rank-and-file prisoners worthy of clemency. But an omnibus bill he signed in his
final months as president, which was mostly aimed at relieving
businesses and individuals hit by the coronavirus pandemic,
also restored Pell grants for incarcerated college students.

The cultural and generational shift away from the punitive was evident in December 2017 when I attended the finale
of a semester-long studio at Yale run by the renowned architect
Frank Gehry. A dozen students had been assigned to solve the
problem that worried the Philadelphia Society for Alleviating
the Miseries of Public Prisons two centuries earlier: design
new, more humane prisons. A jury of experts had assembled to
examine the drawings and maquettes. The students had reimag-
ined prison as a university campus, prison as a health and wellness facility, prison as a monastery, prison as a communal
apartment complex, prison as a summer camp, prison as a tex-
tile workshop (complete with a mulberry orchard to feed the

30   silkworms). Virtually every student incorporated classrooms, open space and fresh air, and inviting places for family visits and therapy. In some of the models, walls were essentially decorative features and staying on-site was more or less optional. It fell to a formerly incarcerated juror, lawyer and poet Reginald Dwayne Betts, to point out the underlying paradox: that if you release the least menacing, those who remain will be the most violent. "You seem to be designing prisons for people who shouldn't be in prison," Betts said.

Some newly galvanized critics rejected the very idea of humane prisons in favor of more radical alternatives to incarceration.

One is "restorative justice," a protocol that—with the blessing of a judge—invites accused individuals and victims into a moderated discussion about the harm done and the best way to make amends. As Danielle Sered has pointed out, decades of studies identify four main conditions that foretell violent behavior: "shame, isolation, exposure to violence, and a diminished ability to meet one's economic needs." Those, she notes, are defining characteristics of life in American prison. Sered, founder of the group Common Justice, works with district attorneys to deal with violent crime (excluding murder and rape) outside the traditional courts-and-corrections system.

"One of the problems with prison," she said, "is that there is never a time in the prisoner's incarceration where they are required to actually grapple with the impact their choices had on other people's lives. . . . We've ended up with a country that is very rich in punishment and very poor in accountability."

Restorative justice requires the cooperation of victims and their families, not to mention willing prosecutors and judges. It is also a labor-intensive, bespoke process, hard to scale up. But variations of this approach have found a toehold in a number of liberal jurisdictions—not only as an alternative to court but as an element of rehabilitation for prisoners already serving time. Prisoners who have been through the program say it helped them understand their motivations and accept responsibility for their crimes.

"You learn to feel remorse, you learn about cycles of violence, you learn about the factors that cause crime," said Juan Moreno Haines, who joined an intensive two-year restorative justice course, the Victim Offender Education Group in San Quentin, California's oldest prison, where he is serving twenty-five to life. After months of introspection guided by a therapist, he told me, comes the main event: "You sit across from a victim of a violent crime and answer their questions—the big one being why it happened to them. For me that was extremely powerful. I have a history of domestic violence, drug abuse, and sexual assault. To actually speak to someone who was victimized, to hear how it impacted their lives, even now I feel that shame."

People who follow criminal justice policy for a living say the fastest growing subset of the burgeoning anti–mass incarceration movement consists of self-described abolitionists who contend a system that is inherently racist and based on retribution should be pulled up by the roots. Activists like Angela Y. Davis of the University of California Santa Cruz and Mariame Kaba of the Barnard Center for Research on Women have attracted a following by calling for a great leap of imagination: a society with no prisons at all.

32   Abolitionists generally start with two ambitious demands. The first is devolving responsibility for public safety to local communities. ("Civilianizing safety," some experts call it.) One reason New York City reduced its crime rate while simultaneously slashing arrests is that the city has a nonprofit network on the ground, some of it subsidized by the city, to combat violence and to help the formerly incarcerated safely reenter society. In April 2021, President Biden proposed, as part of a massive infrastructure bill, to spend $5 billion for community violence–prevention measures.

The other demand is to redistribute government spending from police and prisons to narrow the underlying, crime-breeding inequalities of wealth and opportunity by investing in housing, education, jobs, and health care.

Abolitionists have been shouting from the political fringe for decades, but recently, as Elizabeth Glazer, then director of New York City's criminal justice office, told me, "many of the ideas that animate [the abolitionists] are now finding their way into established criminal justice structures," not just via scholars and activists but via prosecutors questioning what crimes should be prosecuted and judges seeking non-court remedies. Glazer attributes the shift to an awareness that "the criminal justice system can do harm" as well as enhance safety. It can break families, derail careers, and demolish community cohesion. New York's experience, plummeting crime rates alongside declining incarceration rates, seemed to demonstrate the rewards of a lighter touch. People who do not accumulate arrest records and jail time are more likely to stay employed, in families, and out of trouble.

To reformists who work in or with the system, the abolitionists can be exasperating—a case of the ideal being the enemy of the good. DeAnna Hoskins, president of JustLeadershipUSA, which mobilizes former prisoners to press for reform and investment in broken communities, points to the campaign that persuaded New York City to say it would close the notorious jail complex on Rikers Island. The plan depends on building smaller, more humane jails in four boroughs to house a much-reduced population of prisoners. Along with the inevitable not-in-my-backyard resistance, the city has faced vocal opposition from abolitionists who object to *any* new jails on principle.

"That's just not realistic," Hoskins said. She added, "I believe in the end when we talk about abolishing prisons and abolishing law enforcement, [what we mean is] reducing the power and the reach of those entities."

"I don't think that in my lifetime we'll ever abolish prisons, but it's a really important question, why we put people in prisons," said Jeremy Travis, the former president of the John Jay College of Criminal Justice, adding that the abolition debate is "a healthy tension that is really challenging the pace of reform and the status quo."

After all, closing Rikers was a radical idea, until it wasn't. The #cut50 campaign to reduce prison populations by half was mocked as unrealistic until it sank in that this is essentially restoring the incarceration levels of the 1980s.

As I write this in the closing days of 2021, criminal justice reformers are anxiously watching violent crime spike in several American cities, and law-and-order rhetoric is heating

34   up. In December, recently elected mayors in New York and San Francisco—both Black Democrats—were advocating more aggressive policing, London Breed decrying a "reign of criminals" in San Francisco, Eric Adams rethinking the plan to close the Rikers Island jail complex in New York.

It is clear the Trump years have complicated the search for common ground of any kind, and the bipartisan justice agenda is no exception. The momentum of the Black Lives Matter movement—and the Republican tendency to demonize it— cast doubt on whether this improbable alliance would survive the centrifugal forces pulling the electorate apart. Right-wing politicians trafficked in culture-war panic about vast pedophile conspiracies and anti-racist "indoctrination."

In October, Senator Cory Booker, an ardent reformer, reminisced wistfully about working with President Trump's son-in-law, Jared Kushner, and Mark Holden, a lobbyist for the libertarian Koch brothers, to pass the 2018 First Step Act— which passed 87 to 12 in the Senate.

"The rhetoric I hear now—in committee hearings, on the Senate floor—is that violence rates are rising, cities are exploding," Booker said. Trust has evaporated and been replaced by tribalism.

"The Republican Party is the party of Trump now," Booker said. "There are great Republicans out there who believe strongly in these issues, but I think the space in which they can operate and still have political viability is narrowing."

By the waning days of the Trump administration, even Pat Nolan, writing in the *American Conservative*, was promulgating a favorite right-wing conspiracy theory—that billionaire George Soros was masterminding a "Trojan horse" strategy to elect

soft-on-crime prosecutors and bring down the entire criminal
justice system. Soros was helping to bankroll the campaigns of
several district attorney candidates whose anti—mass incarceration agenda might have found sympathy on the reformist right
before the lockstep partisanship of Trump Republicans.

"Soros and his network of wealthy radicals believe the
criminal justice system is so corrupt, so hopelessly racist, that
justice is literally impossible," Nolan wrote. "They have little
interest in reforming the system. Instead, they want to destroy
it from within."

Whether this is the pent-up distress of pandemic isolation
or the beginning of another punitive turn remains to be seen.

The Science of Crime and Punishment

Over the course of the 1990s, crime rates in America fell by more than one-third. This abrupt change lowered the ambient level of public anxiety about crime and emboldened reformers. But why did it happen? One of my colleagues at the Marshall Project, Dana Goldstein, set out to explain. We called her piece "Ten (Not Entirely Crazy) Theories Explaining the Great Crime Decline."

One of the more improbable theses Dana examined was that after *Roe v. Wade* the legalization of abortion meant fewer unwanted children—children who, owing to neglect, would be more likely to break the law. In a similar vein, other researchers have surmised that removing brain-damaging lead from paint and fuel made for a less "criminogenic" environment. Another theory gave credit to technology: anti-theft devices in cars, home alarm systems, and the spread of online banking made us less vulnerable to thieves. Some criminologists theorized that the large baby boom generation simply aged out of crime, which tends to be a young person's game. Most experts gave some

credit to the increased deployment and equipping of police, to
a healthy economy with low unemployment, and to the waning
popularity of crack cocaine. And, of course, some of the decline
was a result of the fact that more bad guys were locked up—the
upside of mass incarceration, if you will. Some studies indi-
cated that getting more criminals off the streets accounted for
as much as a quarter of the great decline, albeit at a high price.

As Dana's reporting demonstrated, explaining the interaction between crime and punishment—the causes and effects,
the costs and benefits—is an inexact science. Some of the
research is based on dubious assumptions or on small or unrep-
resentative samples. Some is colored by ideology.

The US criminal justice "system" is in reality hundreds of
largely autonomous systems—a federal system, fifty state systems, some 18,000 local systems. They may have different defi-
nitions of what constitutes grand larceny or aggravated assault,
and different rates of reporting by victims. There is little consistent sharing of data or correlating of experiences. Prisons,
moreover, come in myriad varieties: urban and remote, public
and privately run, men's, women's, and juveniles', with security
levels ranging from "Club Fed" to supermax. Jails, which hold
those awaiting trial and serving short time, can resemble your
worst nightmare or your Holiday Inn, depending on whether
you're talking about the bedlam of Los Angeles County's Twin
Towers Correctional Facility or the more comfortable facilities
in neighboring Beverly Hills and Seal Beach. Some prisons offer
abundant rehabilitative programs, while others—and most
jails—offer few to none. It's a truism of corrections: if you've
seen one prison, you've seen one prison.

38   Even a question as seemingly straightforward as what prison costs depends on what you count. A commonly cited estimate of the price of maintaining the country's prisons and jails is $80 billion a year. If you throw in health and pension benefits for prison staff, the cost to governments is more like $90 billion— roughly $45,000 per inmate per year. A few years ago, a team led by a doctoral student at Washington University in St. Louis, looking beyond the dollars spent on building and staffing cell blocks, attempted to put a price on the "social costs" of incarceration. They estimated the lost wages, the costs to family members of visitation, the higher mortality rates of both former inmates and their infant children, child welfare payments, evictions and relocations, divorces, diminished property values, and the increased criminality of children with incarcerated parents. The grand total they came up with was $1 *trillion* a year, $450,000 per inmate.

So you've been warned. Be wary of experts who aren't at least a little ambivalent about their conclusions.

Jeremy Travis, who has spent decades steeped in the evidence-driven, data-based study of crime, cautions against "worshipping the false gods of randomized control trials." Along with the question of what works, he says "we should ask questions like what's the right thing to do? What meets the test of human dignity? What's consistent with our democracy?"

Scholars think of prisons as having four main purposes: punishment (society evens the score), incapacitation (putting criminals where they can do no harm to the general public), deterrence (a warning to the tempted that there will be consequences), and rehabilitation (preparing offenders to be law-abiding citizens).

Mountains of research have been devoted to assessing how well
prisons fulfill those objectives.

Of the four rationales for imprisonment, punishment is the most subjective and the hardest to calibrate.

Justice Potter Stewart summed up the case for punishment in *Gregg v. Georgia*, the 1976 Supreme Court ruling reinstating the death penalty: "The instinct for retribution is part of the nature of man, and channeling that instinct in the administration of criminal justice serves an important purpose in promoting the stability of a society governed by law. When people begin to believe that organized society is unwilling or unable to impose upon criminal offenders the punishment they 'deserve,' then there are sown the seeds of anarchy"—including "vigilante justice, and lynch law."

But what does a lawbreaker "deserve"? What is enough? Punishment is not utilitarian; it is an end in itself, a balancing of the scales. As the University of Cincinnati criminologist Francis Cullen points out, punishment assumes that a crime was an act of free will for which the offender should be held accountable by suffering harm at least equal to the harm inflicted. In his textbook (written with Cheryl Lero Jonson) *Correctional Theory: Context and Consequences*, Cullen asks, what if crime is not entirely the product of free will? "[W]hat if criminological research shows—as indeed it does—that the propensity for crime begins in the first years of life and that offenders are, through no conscious choice of their own, quite different from non-offenders?"

If your rationale for putting people in prison is punitive, Cullen added in an interview, you have some obligation to make the punishment proportionate to the offense.

40 Sentencing an offender to forfeit years of freedom may seem a fair consequence, but the scales tip toward injustice when you add in all the collateral suffering common in prison—the tormenting of the weak by the strong, the separation of families, the mind-wrecking loneliness of solitary confinement, and, as we have been reminded by the coronavirus pandemic, the risk of disease.

Incapacitation, at first glance, is the most practical justification for locking people up. A criminal removed from the streets can't harm us (assuming the *us* excludes fellow prison residents and staff). Scholars have attempted to put a dollar value on incapacitation by weighing the cost of incarceration against the cost of the crimes an offender *would have committed* if he remained at large. This entails a great deal of guesswork. Back in the Reagan era a Justice Department economist named Edwin Zedlewski calculated that each criminal added to the prison population would cost the taxpayers $25,000 a year to confine, but would save the nation $430,000 in crimes avoided. Zedlewsky's conclusions were mocked by criminologists who showed that, using Zedlewsky's assumptions, the rising tide of incarceration should have eliminated crime entirely by 1986. But the exaggerated value of incapacitation remained an article of faith among tough-on-crime enthusiasts. (One was William P. Barr, who, in his first tour as US attorney general in 1992, issued a working paper called "The Case for More Incarceration," which framed a stark choice: more prisons or more crime.)

A more dispassionate expert, William Spelman, an urban policy specialist at the University of Texas, in a painstaking review of the scientific literature, concluded that "selective incapacitation"—focused on the most serious and persistent

offenders—would reduce crime, but only by a few percentage
points.

"Society will continue to incapacitate criminals, and selective policies can help to make incapacitation more effective; but the crime problem can never be substantially reduced through incapacitation alone," Spelman said.

And whatever safety dividend is achieved by incapacitation stops when a prisoner is released—as most prisoners are, sooner or later.

As for the idea that prison—the experience of it or the threat of it—is a deterrent, it assumes potential offenders pause to consider the risks versus the gains of their crimes. Research points to a few important holes in this theory. For one thing, much criminal behavior is spontaneous, or nearly so, seizing an opportunity, acting on a drunken impulse, reacting to an insult, or going along with a group. And when an offender does weigh the risks, the risk that looms largest by far is the chance of being caught. The penalty for being convicted might be more or less severe, but if the offender thinks the chance of being caught is slight, the severity of the punishment has little deterrent effect.

Some research suggests that, rather than deterring future crime, prison makes it more likely.

David J. Harding, a UC Berkeley sociologist, followed two groups of men convicted of similar violent crimes (mostly robbery and assault), some of whom, by the luck of the draw, were sentenced to short prison terms and some of whom got probation. The study found that, once released, the incarcerated men were at least as likely as the men on probation to be arrested and convicted of new violent felonies. "These results suggest that

42   for individuals on the current policy margin between prison and probation, imprisonment is an ineffective long-term intervention for violence prevention, as it has, on balance, no rehabilitative or deterrent effects after release," Harding and his research colleagues reported in the journal *Nature Human Behaviour*.

A 2021 report in the journal *Crime and Justice* examined 116 studies of the comparative effects of prison versus "noncustodial sanctions" such as probation, and declared the findings amounted to a "criminological fact." "Incarceration cannot be justified on the grounds it affords public safety by decreasing recidivism. Prisons are unlikely to reduce reoffending unless they can be transformed into people-changing institutions."

Bruce Western, now teaching at Columbia, went a step further in *Punishment and Inequality in America*, marshalling an array of research indicating that "some of those released from prison may be more likely to be involved in crime, *because they were incarcerated* [italics his]." One version of this argument suggests that prison serves as "a school for criminals, surrounding first-timers with those who have spent many years in the criminal justice system." (The schooling he has in mind is not so much lockpicking technique or the comparative merits of firearms as a to-hell-with-the-rules attitude.) Another variation holds that prison "undermines economic opportunity and family stability," lowering prospects for a successful reentry to society. Of course, both versions may be true.

"The theories of deterrence and incapacitation resonate with common sense," Western observed. "If you lock up criminals, they can't commit crime. If penalties are severe, potential criminals will be unwilling to take the risk. The reality is more complicated."

That leaves rehabilitation. Much research indicates that   43
the right kind of therapeutic intervention makes the public
safer. That in turn repays the treasury by restoring offenders to
society as productive, taxpaying citizens and obviating the need
to construct and operate so many prisons.

The conventional measure of rehabilitation is recidivism:
Does the subject sin again after being released? It is a slippery
metric. Some studies define recidivism as a new arrest, while
others count only new convictions or an actual return to prison.
Some of those who do go back to prison did not commit serious
crimes but got caught in technical violations of probation or
parole—failed drug tests, missed appointments, broken curfews. And it's not easy to connect cause and effect. For example,
inmates who enroll in college courses in prison are not a random
sample of the imprisoned population; so if they keep to the
straight and narrow after release, is that really a rehabilitative benefit of higher education, or just indicative of a stronger
character?

Some experts—particularly prison educators—would
prefer to measure progress by more qualitative tests. Some use
post-release interviews to track family dynamics, career satis-
faction, and other signs of healthy reintegration to society.

Still, as an argument to sway voters and their elected officials, the promise of lower recidivism—greater safety, and
possibly for less money—is probably an easier sell than more
abstract justifications.

Whether in practice our system lives up to that promise, how
well it rehabilitates is another question. According to the Bureau
of Justice Statistics, 68 percent of prisoners released from state
prisons are rearrested within nine years. The bureau's data does

44   not consider whether those arrested were subsequently convicted or reincarcerated. A 2015 study by two Oxford scholars who tracked down data from eighteen countries set out to fill that gap. They calculated that in the United States 45 percent of released prisoners were convicted of new crimes within three years and 36 percent returned to prison in that time frame. The researchers said the data was not consistent enough to compare the US with other countries, but, by any measure, there is much room for improvement.

So, what works? Even Robert Martinson, the apostle of the "nothing works" doctrine, didn't quite say that nothing works. In his influential essay in the conservative journal the *Public Interest,* if you read carefully, Martinson found that some programs seemed to cut recidivism rates and some didn't. He concluded that nothing worked *reliably* or *predictably,* not that nothing worked at all.

The challenge for proponents of rehabilitation is to identify measures that work and figure out how to improve the chances of success.

The prevailing model of rehabilitation in US corrections (which draws heavily on a large body of Canadian research) is called RNR, for risk-need-responsivity. Jargon aside, the logic seems sensible. "Risk" means that the most effective interventions target offenders with the highest risk of recidivism, rather than plucking the lowest-hanging fruit. "Need" emphasizes that reductions in recidivism can be achieved by targeting factors known to predict recidivism. Antisocial attitudes and behavior top the list of things that need attention: weak

self-control, anger and resentment, association with other
criminals. "Responsivity" means treatment should be tailored
to the individual learning styles, abilities, and characteristics of
the participants.

The goal, said Cullen, is "to have offenders learn a set of
behavioral and cognitive skills—such as how to think differently, how to control anger and impulsivity, how to avoid criminal associates, and how to respond in prosocial rather than
antisocial ways when in risky situations (e.g., insulted in a bar,
seeing an unguarded computer)."

The most effective weapons in the reform arsenal are cognitive behavioral programs, like teaching prisoners to deal with
anger, but Cullen also sees strong evidence for occupational
programs, substance abuse counseling, and education. Programs that are unstructured tend not to work; programs that are
punitive "never work."

"To be fair," he concedes, "rehabilitation has its own challenges to overcome if it is to claim the mantle as the guiding
theory of corrections. For one thing, it is not easy to change
people who do not want to change and may have spent their
whole lives developing into hardcore criminals. Further, saving
people within correctional agencies is difficult. Prisons are
hardly ideal therapeutic settings, and many correctional workers
lack the professional orientation, therapeutic expertise, and
organizational resources to deliver effective interventions."

But with 95 percent of the prison population destined to be
released at some point, Cullen depicts rehabilitation as not only
an investment in public safety but a moral imperative. To have
people "within the grasp of the correctional system for years on

46   end" and then release them untreated is a dereliction of duty. He calls for "a renewed social purpose in corrections—originally articulated by the founders of the American penitentiary—to forfeit the easy policy of warehousing the wicked in favor of the more difficult but noble policy of saving the wayward."

The Upside-Down Kingdom

On the phone from his involuntary home in the state prison at Otisville, New York, Kayron Jackson wanted to read me something. Jackson has been in and out of state custody—mostly in—since he was fifteen. When we connected he was approaching his forty-sixth birthday, serving twenty-five years to life for murder and burglary, his third conviction. He had spent years establishing a prison reputation as a dangerous man to mess with; he'd joined the Bloods, the dominant Black gang in New York lockups, collected some scars but held his own in the guerilla warfare of the yard, and earned months of punitive isolation in the SHU, the segregated housing unit. Gradually he had shifted allegiance to a different crew, whose gang colors are long sleeves, neatly creased pants, and notebooks. He'd become a programmer, collecting certificates for completing self-improvement programs. He had earned fourteen diplomas, including courses on parenting skills and AIDS awareness, and a high school equivalency degree. His first shot at parole comes in 2023.

48   What Jackson wanted to read to me was a tract called "The Upside-Down Kingdom," which evolved from a New Testament trope and serves some prisoners the way the "Serenity Prayer" serves recovering addicts—an appeal to our better selves. The version Jackson recited to me went like this:

> Anyone with half a sound mind entering a prison environment will soon discover that prisoners govern themselves by codes and rules that counter their own best interests. In prison an arrogant man convicted of killing is respected above the intellectual, sophisticated man or prisoner with moral conviction. . . . In prison you can't afford to smile too broadly or too often. . . . In prison a prisoner is mocked and counted a traitor if he talks about turning over a new leaf and legitimizing his life, is ridiculed if he desires to become a faithful family man and maintain employment to provide for his household. The prisoner is frowned upon when he devotes his energy toward education or acquiring vocational skills above wasting decades playing basketball in the yard. . . . Ideally, prisoners should fill correctional institution educational classes until they are bursting at the seams. . . . If we prisoners were working with sober mental clarity, our prison environments could be transformed into universities of higher learning, or monasteries to obtain deeper insight and spirituality.

While immersing myself in the science of rehabilitation, I was also turning for a reality check to people who have lived it, a kind of informal focus group of incarcerated and formerly incarcerated men and women I've encountered who seemed to have found purpose.

I've warned against generalizing about prisons ("When you've seen one prison...") but my little focus group has resided cumulatively in dozens of correctional facilities. I sent out an invitation: "Judging by recidivism rates, we do a pretty mediocre job of preparing the incarcerated for life after prison—rehabilitation. Imagine the correctional powers-that-be reached out and asked for your advice: what's the best thing (or two or three) we could do in prison to improve the chances of a successful return to the free world?"

Most of my sample could identify programs that helped steer them straight: for John J. Lennon, a creative writing class in Attica; for Juan Moreno Haines, who is serving time in San Quentin, a restorative justice group that includes encounters with victims of violence; for Joseph Spinks, a lifer in Chester, Pennsylvania, a program that trains abandoned puppies for adoption. But no one described this as a sudden road-to-Damascus conversion.

"Change comes about when you're tired," Jackson said. "When you're tired of running into the wall. When you're tired of being hurt. You can make all the programs you want; if the individual is not ready to make that effort, nothing is going to happen."

Almost without exception my sources echoed criminologist Francis Cullen's cautions about rehabilitation: it is not easy to change people who do not want to change, and most prisons are hardly ideal therapeutic settings, lacking the professional

50   orientation, expertise, and resources to successfully intervene in troubled lives. The advice from inside was mostly about context, about culture, not content.

One recurring complaint was that corrections systems often wait until prisoners are on the brink of release to sign them up for programs aimed at restoring them safely to society. "A lot of these programs won't take you in until you've got one foot out the door," said Jonathan Andujar, who spent thirteen years in the prisons and jails of New York. By then it's often too late; prisoners have been steeped in the cynical outlook of the upside-down kingdom.

"Attempting to prepare an individual for reentry to society after twenty or more years in prison by running them through a three- or six-month program is futile," says Aaron Flaherty, who is serving a life sentence in Texas for driving the getaway car in a convenience store robbery-murder. Charting an individual's course to reentry "should start from Day One."

Back in 2016, Flaherty, assisted by four other Texas prisoners, compiled a remarkable sixty-five-page package of advice on how to orient prisons toward rehabilitation. Some of the topics were obvious, such as family visits (more of them, longer and less dreary) and accessing technology (basic computer literacy is a prerequisite for life in the free world), along with some less obvious, such as the role of chaplains (they should get out of their offices and mingle) and dentures (apparently Texas makes many toothless prisoners gum their meals).

Flaherty's advice begins at the beginning, with intake:

When inmates arrive at a transfer facility, they are taken from the bus and walked to the entrance of the facility.

Immediately they are yelled at by officers to strip naked, get "nuts to butts," and after being searched they are kept naked for several minutes until they are issued some boxers. . . . During this process, officers are yelling obscenities at the inmates. . . . This demoralizing routine seeks obedience but provides no direction or guidance to the inmate. . . . Intake is the first opportunity to rehabilitate, and as such this stage should be taken more seriously. New arrivals should have counseling available and should receive immediate training to prepare them for the prison culture and to inoculate them against gang recruiters, extortion, and other threats.

Five years later, Flaherty expanded his manual into a book. Sadly for prison inhabitants, he won't have to change much. He noted one promising development, the fact that many prisons are making available digital tablets that can access educational materials and other approved content, though the open internet is still off-limits and some purveyors charge exorbitant rates for tablet service. As a rule, he says, prison administrators are more likely to speak the language of rehabilitation these days, but too little of it trickles down to the frontline staff.

Prison veterans say corrections should make better use of the human capital at hand: the inmates. Programs that get people to examine their thinking and behavior are fine, but more effective when facilitated by fellow prisoners. "Inmate-to-inmate," Flaherty said, "you get men who have changed their lives reaching out to the men who want different, but they just don't know how to do different." Both the veterans and the novices benefit. Prisoners with distant or no prospect of release can still

52   be enlisted as mentors, tutors, or counselors. Flaherty won't be eligible for parole until 2036, but he got his high school equivalency in county jail, and while in state prisons earned two associate degrees and a bachelor of science in biblical studies from Southwestern Baptist Theological Seminary. He is certified as a nondenominational field minister. He now spends his days counseling a wing of eighty-four fellow prisoners on everything from renouncing gangs to writing resumes. "It's called a faith-based dorm, but it's more of a life skills academy."

"The more I educated myself," he said, "the more I realized that life doesn't have to be just misery, that even in prison we can live life with a purpose."

But too often, prisoners told me, a history of misconduct—even ten years in the past—can disqualify a prisoner from leading a class or serving as a counselor.

"If a guy is trying to teach a class about [controlling] violence," Jackson said, "if he comes from a violent past—and he's no longer about that—he's a perfect candidate to teach other prisoners." Since joining the programmers, Jackson has been a facilitator or teacher in several programs.

A recurring theme in my conversations was that corrections should rely more on incentives and less on mandates. I heard considerable scorn for the drug treatment and anger management programs that many prisons make a prerequisite for release. Too often prisoners enrolled in these mandatory programs—and the instructors—are just going through the motions. Programs that are voluntary, on the other hand, demonstrate and encourage some initiative.

Some prisons have honors units where inmates who follow   53
the rules have more freedoms, and there is often an opportunity
to earn a reduction in sentence for good behavior, but in many
places the only reward for self-improvement is the absence of
punishment.

"Giving inmates the ability to set themselves apart from
those who choose to continue to misbehave would give an
inmate a reason to care about his future," Flaherty says. "It
would give him hope that his future can be different; and giving
inmates hope about a better future will change the culture of the
prison system."

John J. Lennon, who is twenty years into a twenty-eight-
to-life sentence in New York for murder, argues that the culture should change from the top, starting with superintendents. Lennon, a largely self-taught journalist with whom I have
worked on stories about life inside, contends prison administrators are too disengaged.

"The fact that prison administrators don't lean into relationships with prisoners is itself the problem," he told me in an
email. "It's why superintendents of prisons should be PhDs in
criminology or psychology, not former guards who've worked
their way up the ranks. These new superintendents would build
better relationships with prisoners. I think these scholars will
also understand that they can't help us themselves but that
their job would be to create a culture in which rehabilitation can
be had. . . . Rehabilitation happens within the prisoner ranks.
Administrators have to empower and nurture relationships.
In my two decades in prison, I have never had an encouraging
conversation with a corrections administrator. Nor have I been

54   inspired by any of them. But many of my peers have inspired me over the years."

Wilfredo Laracuente, recently paroled from Sing Sing after twenty years for killing a rival drug dealer, said even when the administration is relatively progressive, as it is in Sing Sing, the attitude doesn't always trickle down to frontline corrections officers. Laracuente's short list of recommendations includes retraining the staff.

Almost every conversation I had with prison veterans turned sooner or later to a plea for respect, for dignity.

"Treat people like people," said Keri Blakinger, who spent nearly two years in the custody of the state of New York for being caught with six ounces of heroin. "If you treat people like objects, animals, or numbers, you cannot make them better at being people."

When Kayron Jackson talks fondly about a program called Alternatives to Violence, what seems to impress him is not so much the curriculum but the attitude of the volunteers, mostly white women in their sixties. "It's humbling to have these older women showing us that we're loved and we're cared for. They're not standing six feet away like we've got COVID. They're not talking down to us."

"Humane treatment from officers and other staff members increases public safety, promotes positive behavior among inmates, helps prisoners reintegrate back into society, and reduces the number of new victims," says Flaherty's guide to reform. But in the upside-down culture of incarceration, respect is regarded as weakness.

Flaherty recalls that not long ago a new corrections officer who arrived fresh out of the military was reprimanded for

addressing prisoners as "sir." When Flaherty asked why, a CO   55
told him, "When we address you as sir, we make you our equal,
and we are not to make you our equal in any way."

"Do you know *Les Miserables*?" Flaherty asked me. "Jean
Valjean says—and I'm paraphrasing—'Sir' to a convict is like a
cup of cold water to a parched man."

The Normality Principle

Over the past decade, American prison reform advocates have organized field trips for American corrections officials to study how their European counterparts use prisons. Scandinavia and Germany have been favorite destinations, and more than a few American officials say the experience led to an epiphany. That these countries lock up far fewer people for much shorter sentences than we do in the United States was, to these insiders, not news. How they treat those they *do* incarcerate was, to anyone familiar with American prisons, mind-blowing.

In 2015, we sent a Marshall Project staff writer, Maurice Chammah, to Germany on a trip organized by the Vera Institute of Justice, a New York–based think tank that promotes criminal justice reform. The travelers included the heads of the prison systems in New Mexico, Washington, Tennessee, and Connecticut, several district attorneys, corrections officers, and Connecticut's then-governor Dannel P. Malloy.

"Germany's system," Maurice wrote, "serves as a reference point for reflecting on the punitive mentality that has come to define the US justice system."

I talked to Michael P. Lawlor, a Connecticut state lawmaker and professor of criminal justice, who joined that trip as an advisor to Governor Malloy. He remembers the excursion as transformative.

"We went to a maximum-security prison outside Berlin," Lawlor told me. "There's like a thirty-foot wall. Our bus goes in and it's like a brand-new community college campus—glass corridors, carpets on the floor. Nobody's wearing any kind of uniform, just name tags to indicate who's a prisoner, who's a staff person. They take us into the quote-unquote cell blocks, they're more or less like college dorm rooms, with real doors and stuff. A big window, curtains, a desk, a chair, a private bathroom with its own shower. The prisoners have keys to their own rooms. This is really something.

"So we're walking down the hall and there's like this big glass-enclosed room and one of the American corrections guys says, 'What's that?' A German guy says, 'It's a kitchen. If they don't want to go down to the dining area they can prepare their own meals.' And the American guy says, 'There's knives in there.' And the German guy says, 'Yeah, it's a kitchen, what do you expect?' The American guy says, 'Well, how often do you have an incident?' 'What do you mean by incident?' 'You know, somebody gets stabbed or something.' And the German guy looked at the American like he was crazy: 'We've been open five years and nothing like that has ever happened.'"

The other revelation for Americans is the role of the staff, who in western Europe are viewed less as jailors and more as therapists or social workers. American correctional officers are trained for a few weeks, with a heavy emphasis on how to keep control. In Germany, aspiring prison officers study for two

58   intensive years, including college-level courses in psychology, ethics, and communications skills. COs in the United States are cautioned to avoid personal connection to inmates, even being on a first-name basis, in order to maintain discipline. American visitors to Europe are amazed to see guards—unarmed—shooting baskets, playing chess, sharing lunch, and deep in personal conversation with prisoners. In the US, prison work ranks near the bottom in the caste system of law enforcement. The stress of the job leaves a wake of divorce, alcoholism, PTSD, and suicide. Recruiting and retention are chronic problems. In Germany, corrections jobs are in great demand. Only about 10 percent of applicants make it into the training program, a figure Americans associate with admissions to elite universities.

I heard similar stories from visitors to Norway—which actively proselytizes for its model of corrections and has become the most popular destination for prison exchanges—and other western European countries. Invariably, they describe the purpose of prison as preparing offenders to rejoin society, because most of them will.

That mission entails a few guiding principles.

First, the punishment for crime is deprivation of liberty, period. In all other respects incarcerated people retain their rights as citizens: the right to be safe, the right to education and health care, the right to vote, the right to a measure of privacy, the right (literally enshrined in the German constitution) to dignity.

Second, the job of the correctional system is to diagnose the factors that led an inmate into crime—lack of employable skills, mental health issues, substance abuse, antisocial attitudes—and try to correct them.

Third, the best way to prepare prisoners for normal life is to
maintain, as much as possible, a semblance of normal routines
in prison. "Residents," as the prisoners are usually called, get up
when their alarm goes off, fix breakfast, and head off to work or
school. They are paid a decent wage for their labor (and obliged
to save a portion so they don't leave prison penniless). Under
what is called "the normality principle," they are entitled to rec-
reation, social interaction, regular family contact (including
conjugal visits), even fresh air and gardens.

Even kitchen knives. To American prison officers, every
tool is a potential weapon, private bathrooms are an invitation
to rape or suicide, trees are escape ladders. Jan R. Strømnes,
deputy warden at the Halden maximum security prison in
Norway, recalled the reaction of his prison officers when Halden
was new: "'Oh, it's dangerous,' some of the officers said when we
opened. 'What if the inmates climb up the trees?' 'Well,' we said,
'let them climb up the trees. When they get tired they'll come
down again. There's nowhere to go.'"

Strømnes and other European corrections officials describe
the management of violence as "dynamic security," based on
constant dialogue and a lot of surveillance.

"The point is, our staff knows the inmates," he says. "They
interact so closely that we pick up the signals if anyone is having
trouble."

When "dynamic security" isn't enough, the Europeans use
monetary fines, temporary loss of privileges, cancelation of fur-
loughs, and, in acute situations: isolation. This last resort is in
many American prisons essentially a first resort. Strømnes says
isolation is not regarded as a punishment, as in the US, but a
way to regain control when a prisoner becomes a danger.

60   The Norwegians seem to have strong public support for their approach, which grew out of government white papers in the late twentieth century after a surge of violence and drug abuse in prisons. Brie Williams, a physician and founder of a California-based prison reform group called Amend, recalls that on her first visit to Oslo she struck up a conversation with her taxi driver, who told her it is judges' role to sentence and prison's role to correct: "In Norway people go to court to get punished, they go to prison to become better neighbors." When she heard precisely the same talking point from her waiter that night at dinner, she realized that Norway had not only created a theoretical framework for their approach to corrections, they had apparently found an effective way to sell it to the public.

Probably the ultimate test of public support for Norway's prison philosophy was the case of Anders Breivik. A virulent right-wing extremist, Breivik slaughtered seventy-seven people in July 2011—eight with a bomb in Oslo, then sixty-nine more, most of them teenagers, gunned down at a Labour Party youth camp. Breivik got the maximum sentence—twenty-one years (though he can be held indefinitely if a judge deems him still a threat to society). He is confined in isolation from the general prison population. But this is isolation Norway-style.

"When you [Americans] think of isolation, you have a small concrete cell where you are inside for twenty-three hours every day," Jan Strømnes told me. Breivik, like any Norwegian kept in solitary, has quarters that would pass for a starter apartment in New York, with a living room, a study room, and an exercise room. "He has staff around him all day. He has access to counselors, religious services. So he has a lot of people around him, but he doesn't have other incarcerated people around him."

"He's a student at the university," Strømnes added. "He votes when there's an election, like everybody else."

(One right he does not enjoy is Facebook. European prisons, like their American counterparts, strictly limit internet access for fear that social media and unrestricted email could be used to intimidate witnesses, troll victims, plot new crimes, or otherwise make trouble.)

Imagine the political apoplexy if an American mass killer was confined in such conditions. But in Norway even parents who lost children in Breivik's rampage appeared to be satisfied with the outcome, seeing it as fair punishment that would allow the country, perhaps, to move past its trauma, the *New York Times* reported. "The sense that Mr. Breivik's hateful beliefs should not be allowed to fill Norway with hate, too, was part of the country's response to the attacks from the beginning," the *Times* wrote.

"We do have of course dangerous inmates in Norway," Strømnes said, "but the vast majority are, I would say, non-violent and non-dangerous. We can't make up a system based on the few. We create a system based on the many and we take the necessary actions when needed."

Enough Norwegians?

There is a self-deprecating Russian joke from Soviet days about the minister of agriculture touring the lush farms and bountiful greenhouses of Sweden.

"My God! If only we could do this!" the Russian moans to his Swedish host.

"But why can't you?"

"Not enough Swedes."

I thought of this often when confronted with the way our European allies do prison. Why can't American prisons be more like Norway's? Not enough Norwegians?

Norway is a prosperous, relatively centralized, relatively homogeneous society, with a my-brother's-keeper social welfare culture. The US is a fractured country that mythologizes individualism and tends to treat poverty as a failure of personal responsibility. In Europe, firearms are strictly regulated, while America has more civilian-held guns than civilians. Germans and Norwegians insulate their institutions of justice from shifts in public opinion, which the United States, to say the least, does not. Europeans consider it scandalous that in many American jurisdictions judges are expected to woo voters, sometimes by pandering to vengeful moods. In Europe the judges are legal technocrats, usually appointed after vetting by the professional bar.

"Our most important friend is not the politicians, not the society, it's our federal constitutional court," said Susanne Gerlach, who oversees the prison system in Berlin. "The court stands up for the goal of rehabilitation, the idea of human dignity."

Despite the political and cultural obstacles, reformers in several American states have set out to adopt elements of European corrections. One approach is to carve out enclaves within existing prisons and create small demonstration projects, hoping to expand them.

Scott Semple, as Connecticut's corrections chief, made several excursions to Germany and Norway, including that 2015 trip with his boss, Governor Malloy. Malloy's administration had already been pushing to limit mandatory sentences and improve job opportunities for released prisoners. Upon their return from Germany, Semple created an experimental unit within the traditional, hard-time maximum security prison in the town of Cheshire. Semple focused on young adults, eighteen to twenty-five, the cohort statistically most likely to return to a life of crime. About fifty young adults were joined by a cadre of older prisoners serving as mentors.

Maurice Chammah visited the experiment, dubbed TRUE, in 2018 and described the atmosphere as "somewhere between family and reformatory, with strict rules, incentives, and long

64   days of work and study. The young men go through a series of stages, learning to confront their pasts, to be vulnerable around their peers, to resolve conflicts through communication instead of violence, and to master basic life skills they may have missed, such as managing a personal budget."

TRUE was credited with reducing violence in the prison, and none of the first nine men paroled from the program had ended up back in prison, but the sample was still small and the program was still young.

The Vera Institute, which helped Connecticut develop TRUE, is setting up similar young adult programs in Massachusetts and South Carolina—although there have been setbacks due to COVID-19. Connecticut also has a similar program, called WORTH, at the state's women's prison.

But Malloy and Semple, who championed the more European approach, are gone now. Angel Quiros, a thirty-year corrections professional who succeeded Semple as director of the Connecticut system, told me he was facing budget cuts that would total $150 million over five years, shutting three prisons and slashing payroll. He said he expects to protect the TRUE and WORTH units but sees little opportunity to expand them. "Those units are heavily, heavily staffed," he said. "This is not the right timing." He supports the programs, but believes what happens in prison has less bearing on crime than what happens before, such as schooling and child health, and after, such as employment and housing—none of which are the responsibility of the corrections department.

Cost is one of the biggest obstacles to replicating Norwegian corrections practices, according to those who have tried. Staffing levels in Germany are about two employees (officers, counselors, medical personnel) for every three residents. In Norway the ratio approaches one-to-one. According to the Bureau of Justice Statistics, state prisons in the US typically operate on a prisoner-staff ratio of five-to-one, and federal prisons more than ten-to-one.

John Wetzel, who as Pennsylvania director of corrections was a member of that German prison tour delegation, recalled visiting the German youth facility. "We have a facility with a similar purpose [in Pennsylvania]," he told me in early 2021. "Our square footage is almost identical. But they had a third of the population with the same number of staff. That encapsulates the limiting factor to scaling the European approach: it's expensive."

"The way to scale it in our political and financial environment," Wetzel continued," is to build pockets of it, show success, and then keep expanding the pockets."

Wetzel's first pocket, dubbed Little Scandinavia, was a housing unit within the medium-security state prison at Chester, Pennsylvania, chosen in part for the facility's emphasis on rehabilitation, especially addiction therapy. The project is "closer to the Scandinavian model than probably any other unit in the country," according to Jordan Hyatt, a Drexel University criminologist who is monitoring and advising the Chester experiment along with a partner from the University of Oslo, Synøve Andersen.

The living quarters were repurposed to resemble a campus lounge, with new furniture, fresh paint, some planters and a fish tank, a full kitchen (yes, with knives, though tethered to the counter), a washer and dryer. The cells are single-occupant, with small flat-screens and mini-fridges. The heart of the program is a large enough staff to allow for engagement: 4 officers per shift overseeing 64 prisoners, compared to a single officer for 126 inmates in Chester's general population units. In 2019, while the managers made the rounds of Norway, Sweden, and Denmark, the line officers spent weeks shadowing their counterparts in three Norwegian facilities. To expand the range of job training, the team has reached out to a barista to teach coffee service and a mortician to teach mortuary management. The staff spent months rewriting job descriptions based on their Norwegian experience. In March 2020, the first residents, six prisoners serving life sentences, were moved in to serve as mentors. The administration was poised to select the remaining residents by lottery.

And then the coronavirus pushed the pause button.

Little Scandinavia became a quarantine center for the infected, and then a temporary home for inmates displaced by a fire at a sister prison and by a crippled elevator at Chester.

In Thanksgiving week, 2021, I visited the Chester experiment as it was preparing to relaunch after the long COVID shutdown. I arrived well aware of the reasons for skepticism. Wetzel, the scheme's ranking enthusiast, had recently retired. The officers' union was hostile. The costs—mainly the much higher staffing ratios and the expense of retrofitting conventional prison infrastructure to approximate normal life—raised doubts about how Little Scandinavia could be sustainable, let alone scalable.

Patricia Connor-Council, a former social worker and CO who is the unit manager, recalled that Chester used to have a highly regarded two-year substance abuse program; in a wave of budget cuts the program was slashed to four months and out-sourced to a contractor. "I worry that management is going to renege" on the staffing levels that are essential for the success of the Scandinavia experiment.

But spend a couple of days with the men and women of Little Scandinavia and the project starts to feel not only appealing but plausible.

For one thing, the staff and mentors have an infectious sense of mission. The officers, despite some taunts from their peers, are deeply invested, having been part of every decision down to the color of paint. They have taken to heart the ideals of normality without losing sight of what is politically viable. Pennsylvania, the team reckons, is probably not ready for con-jugal visits—though six other American states have them and they are routine in Europe—or for escorted inmate outings to the shopping mall. A twenty-six-year-old Chester officer named Tyler Karasinski told me that when he was shadowing Norwegian staff in an Oslo prison, "Two guards took six inmates camping. We're like, that's not going to happen here, at least for a while. But the main thing that can happen here is interaction with the inmates. Over there they sit down and play some cards, watch a movie, play basketball, go to the gym with them. . . . Here, if you did that in a regular unit, you'd lose your job."

The team of officers recruited for the project is diverse—about half Black, about half women, a mix of veterans and young officers—and well versed in the lessons of Scandinavia, based on exchanges of staff and lots of Zoom conversations.

Danette Battle, fifty-six, who joined the Chester correctional staff fifteen years ago after retiring from the Navy, spent two weeks in Norway, and at first found it "almost too laid back."

68   By the time she returned, though, she had come to appreciate the Norwegian approach as creating an environment where rehabilitation has a much better chance.

"This is not working, what we're doing here," she told me. "We're going backward. . . . We can do a lot better, and we have to start somewhere."

The six lifers picked as Little Scandinavia mentors are mostly in their fifties and have cumulatively more than 190 years of time spent behind bars. Many have been trained in peer counseling. Pennsylvania—in another Wetzel legacy—has certified hundreds of longtime inmates as peer support specialists, one of a growing number of states that have come to see their incarcerated old guard as an asset. When a prisoner refuses to leave his cell at Chester, before donning body armor for a forced extraction the guards will send in a peer counselor like James Wagstaff to talk the inmate down.

"When I was going up, we didn't have nobody to send in and talk to you before they came in and hit you on the head and dragged you out," said Wagstaff, who is in for second-degree murder, when we chatted in the Little Scandinavia commons.

The Scandinavia team hears plenty of resistance from veteran COs—that this is pampering, that fraternizing with inmates will undermine their authority, even, improbably, that inmates will find the unit so cozy they won't want to leave prison. For prisoners who have lived for years in a cage the size of a parking space, sharing an open toilet with an assigned roommate, the amenities in Little Scandinavia are comparatively luxurious, though hardly up to Norwegian standards. But inmates and officers say it's not mainly about the comforts.

It is, first, about creating a climate of mutual respect; second, about giving prisoners a measure of control over their daily routine; and, third, about lowering the levels of clamor and conflict so that inmates can pay attention to the work of rehabilitation.

The lifer-mentors say the temporary residents sent in during the pandemic lockdown amounted to a dry run, and confirmed their expectations.

"The people who came through here were all races and colors and crimes, you name it—I'm talking the worst of the worst—and they were on their best behavior," Eliezer Perez, one of the mentors, told me. "That's the difference it makes to be treated more humanely and more respectfully."

Perez, sentenced to life for first-degree murder, has spent twenty-six of his forty-eight years in the corrections system. He is an accomplished artist—the walls of Chester are festooned with his murals of civil rights leaders and Mother Teresa—and he uses the unit's communal kitchen to whip up Puerto Rican dishes. "You can cook a meal and sit with the officers and dialogue while you eat," he marveled. "If the Department of Corrections were to switch over to something like this, people would get out of here less angry at the world."

James Wagstaff said the temporary residents who were imported during the pandemic were so accustomed to being compliant that they had lost the ability to make elementary choices—how to organize your day, let alone your life. In this unit the men don't wear uniforms, and are responsible for their own laundry. "These guys had no idea how to iron their own clothes," Wagstaff told me. "If you want to live in society and

70   make right choices, they should be making choices while they're in prison."

The program has promised a rigorous research component, underwritten by Arnold Ventures, a major philanthropic supporter of criminal justice reform, to document the effects on the culture inside, the transition after release, and the (hoped-for) net cost savings. To that end they plan to populate the unit with a random sample of the prison's residents, not just well-behaved residents from the honor block. Jordan Hyatt said he hopes for meaningful results in about two years, after enough prisoners have passed through Little Scandinavia. "As humane or well intentioned as these policies are, they're not going to get traction unless we can show impact," he said. "The graveyards of criminology are littered with well-intentioned programs that didn't work out the way they were supposed to."

An alternative to the pilot project approach is to inject European-style thinking directly into the mainstream of a corrections system.

Reliably red North Dakota (65 percent for Trump in 2020) is probably not the first place you'd look for a model of progressive incarceration. Then again, its low violent crime rate (thirty-second among the states, according to the FBI) creates some political space for reform; its correctional officers—elsewhere often a source of organized resistance—are non-union; and its prison population is manageably small. Oh, and one in three North Dakotans is of Norwegian descent, the highest of any state.

By the time Leann Bertsch, director of the North Dakota Department of Corrections and Rehabilitation, toured prisons in

Europe, she had already begun working with the San Francisco—based reform group Amend, which aims to reimagine prisons as, first and foremost, public health facilities. Their breakthrough reform was limiting the use of solitary confinement throughout the state system. Officials slashed the length of stays in isolation and transformed what had been a typical "administrative segregation" unit, a place to isolate the most disruptive residents for months at a time, into a "behavioral intervention unit," where staff and resident-mentors concentrate on teaching prisoners the interpersonal skills to avoid conflict.

After a visit to Norway in 2015, Bertsch introduced some trappings of normal life. She planted trees and opened the prison grounds for concerts and family barbecues. But rather than carve out an experimental mini-Norway, she mounted a frontal attack on the state's entire system—starting with the recruiting, training, and motivating of prison staff.

"We started to hire people who wanted to be agents of change, not people who wanted to exercise authority," Bertsch told me. The department still hires out of the military (a number have come from Bismarck's large National Guard headquarters), but it now does more recruiting of candidates with college degrees or experience in caregiving professions.

The typical three-week orientation was stretched into three months of structured mentoring, followed by six months of closely supervised probation.

On a late May afternoon, I paid a Zoom visit to the basement training center in Bismarck to eavesdrop as ten new officers went through their final review before beginning their probationary period. After a few breathing and mindfulness exercises, the new officers and trainers played out simulated

72　cell block encounters. One exercise entailed defusing a tense moment between prisoners. ("Hey, bitch, you sitting in *my* seat!") Another required calming a fellow officer who was on the verge of beating up an unruly inmate. Each scenario played out twice, first with the trainers enacting the role of aggressive COs, provoking the trainees playing inmates to respond in kind. Then they traded places, and the trainees became the guards and tried to defuse the situation following the precepts of "dynamic security"—listening, empathizing, offering options, talking them down. (The officers carry no weapons but are drilled in the use of pressure points if a situation "goes hands-on.")

Later I talked to four of the new officers who embodied the more diverse incoming generation of correctional officers: Andre was a twenty-seven-year-old Army vet, following a conventional career path; Jana, thirty-four, had been a counselor at a halfway house after growing up with an addicted and frequently jailed mother; Jaci, forty-two, was a mental health worker; Travis, a twenty-nine-year-old Louisianan, had worked eight months at the notorious Louisiana State Penitentiary in Angola, where the tension was palpable and "the use of force escalated a lot faster" than in North Dakota. I had just watched Travis deftly defuse an impending staff assault on a troublesome inmate in a role-playing exercise. "Sometimes what you need is just somebody to hear what you're saying," he told me.

Bertsch faced dissent from the old guard, who worried that closer interaction with residents would put them in danger. She was mocked for turning prison into "PrisonyLand" or adult day care, for having staff and prisoners mingle at pizza parties and game nights.

Nathan Erickson, a sociologist who interviewed North Dakota prison officers in 2018, found that about half of them had been won over to the new approach, a level of support that has almost certainly grown as the old guard was weeded out.

"They're transitioning from a very different model," Erickson said, "where they would just enforce very strict and specific policies, to one where they're expected to socialize, one where they're supposed to play cards, one where you're supposed to use positive reinforcements when a person is throwing crap at you—literally, crap. For a lot of people that was just beyond the pale." Some were encouraged to take early retirement or find other jobs.

Although data on prisoner behavior is still sketchy, anecdotal evidence and the testimony of people in the system suggest that the atmosphere has become a little more . . . Norwegian. "Positive behavior reports"—which record incidents as seemingly minor as a "good morning" from a chronically sullen resident—have soared. A better indicator may be the way the system mobilized everyone to confront COVID-19: masking, testing, creating quarantine spaces, and freeing low-risk prisoners to avoid crowding. The results, as of July 2021, were astonishing compared to almost all other state prison systems: a total of two deaths (one prisoner, one staffer) and an 80 percent vaccination rate.

In the beginning of the new regime, "I remember feeling unsafe," Daniel Lukach, a corrections officer since 2008, told me. When Bertsch started reducing the use of solitary confinement as a disciplinary tool, "I thought we were putting our people in danger, even putting some residents in danger." Now a lieutenant, Lukach said his sense of danger and constant stress

74 has been replaced by a feeling rarely associated with prison work: pride.

Bertsch had been a prosecutor, served as the corrections chief under three governors, and kept the legislature happy by controlling her budget, so she survived the critics, and her reforms do not appear to be threatened. Her successor, Dave Krabbenhoft, says the department has fully embraced the concept of prison's job as "making better neighbors."

"We've gone from a real narrow definition of public safety, which was making sure the doors were locked and nobody got out, to, now, where we still focus on public safety, but part of it is asking, 'How do we help these people?'"

Bertsch stepped down in 2020, after fifteen years in the job, and now works for a private company that manages prisons in states across the South and Midwest.

"At the end of the day," Bertsch told me, "I'd rather be accused of running adult day care than running a gulag where people come out more angry and more violent."

What's Race Got to Do With It?

One problem Scandinavian prisons don't face on a scale remotely comparable to our own is the toxic legacy of racism. Statistics show that Black men are chronically overrepresented all along the American arc of criminal justice, from stops by police to cells on Death Row. The racial inequity that helps lead so many Black men to prison is also the organizing principle of life inside many prisons. Black, brown, and white gangs—major players like the Bloods, the Nation of Islam, the Latin Kings, and the Aryan Brotherhood, and looser cliques based on neighborhood roots—often operate with the acquiescence or outright encouragement of corrections officials. Prisoners who are not formally embedded in gangs tend to accept the authority of gang leaders over the illicit marketplace in drugs and cell phones and in settling grievances.

"In large prison systems like California, Illinois, New York, and Texas, race is central to the social order of prison," says David Pyrooz, a University of Colorado criminologist

76   who studies prison gangs. The growth of prison populations has made that even more true. For a fearful new arrival seeking security in a crowd of unfamiliar, intimidating faces, race is the obvious identifier.

"You come in, you find your brothers," said Jonathan Andujar, who spent thirteen years in the prisons and jails of New York. "You just gotta be very mindful of who's your enemies, who's watching you, who's snitching. If you got no team behind you, no family behind you—and that's your gang brothers— then you are on your own. It's survival of the fittest."

Andujar found the racial loyalties in prison even stricter than outside. Growing up in Brooklyn, he joined the Bloods and felt fully accepted even though he is Latino and the Bloods are a Black gang. When he connected with the Bloods in the jails of Rikers Island, he was viewed by Latin gangsters with suspicion.

"I grew up in the projects with all races," he told me. "It wasn't about color. When I got locked up I had a rude awakening—my Spanish brothers not accepting me because I'm hanging out with the Blacks. So they look at me like I'm Black. I hadn't realized it's all about races."

Gangs enforce a kind of quasi-military order, but they also contribute to a volatile environment that makes it harder to deliver education, therapy, training, or counseling. Remember the upside-down kingdom: "a prisoner is mocked and counted a traitor if he talks about turning over a new leaf."

In prisons situated hours away from big cities, it is not unusual to find overwhelmingly white local corrections staff supervising overwhelmingly Black and brown prisoners bused in from the metropolis.

"In upstate New York, you have second- and third-generation corrections officers who have never known a Black person who wasn't a convicted felon," said Elizabeth Gaynes, president of the Osborne Association, which assists prisoners in making the transition back to society. Families traveling for hours to visit incarcerated loved ones in such places often feel unwelcome.

"It matters that the people who are the keepers can imagine that the kept could be kin to them," Gaynes told me. "A prerequisite for rehabilitation is recognizing the incarcerated population as fellow humans."

Race continues to distort life after release. For those who have served their time, especially those who return to their old neighborhoods, gangs often offer criminal opportunities on the outside that defeat the purpose of rehabilitation. Andujar opted out of the gang, works as a hospital orderly to support his two kids, and hopes to return to Rikers as a youth counselor, but he said "a lot of people are scared to take that leap of faith, because that gang is all they know."

A 2018 study in North Carolina found Black men are significantly more likely to return to prison, even when they score better on risk assessment tools. The researchers traced 21,462 men and women released from North Carolina state prisons in 2000–2001, comparing factors widely used to calculate the risk of reoffending: age of entry into prison, prior convictions, financial situation, marital status, history of drug use, education level, employment history, and "attitude" (as reported by a corrections official). The researchers suggested that the greater propensity for recidivism among relatively low-risk Black men reflected "pervasive racism and increased surveillance."

78 Remember Pat Nolan's story of guards telling released prisoners, "See you in a few months." For Black men, you might say, recidivism is a self-fulfilling prophesy.

So, is racial inequity the root cause of mass incarceration, a contributing factor, or more of a collateral consequence? How you answer this question may tell you something about how you attempt to set things right. Do we treat these racial disparities as symptoms or as the disease itself?

The prevailing view on the political left was distilled to its essence by the legal scholar Michelle Alexander in her 2010 book, *The New Jim Crow: Mass Incarceration in the Age of Colorblindness*, which shot up the bestseller lists after the 2012 death of Trayvon Martin, a Black teenager shot by a neighborhood watch volunteer in Florida.

The fact that nearly a third of Black men in this country can expect to spend time in jail or prison, Alexander argued, cannot be explained as simply a society defending itself against criminal predators. The War on Crime and the War on Drugs were examples of organized white power defending itself against Black assertiveness.

In her view, Nixon's tough-on-crime agenda and Reagan's escalation of the War on Drugs were aimed, consciously or not, at halting the advances of the civil rights movement and perpetuating the neglect of the underclass. While racism has distorted the administration of justice in this country from its beginning, she says, since the 1980s mass incarceration has decimated minority neighborhoods to the extent that it has become a malign form of containment. "It is no longer concerned primarily with the prevention and punishment of crime, but rather

with the management and control of the dispossessed," she
wrote. She does not shy away from the word "genocide."

The past several decades have provided plenty of circum-
stantial evidence for Alexander's portrayal of systemic racism.
And the system perpetuates itself by voter suppression and
gerrymandering. Incarceration plays a part there too. In every
state except Maine and Vermont, people in prison—and in
most states even people who have served their prison time—are
stripped of their right to vote. In some states this has disenfran-
chised as much as one-fifth of the Black voting-age population.
More subtly, the US census counts prisoners as residents of
their prison's location, not where they come from. Thus, many
rural, largely white prison towns get a greater share of influence
and government largesse thanks to a non-voting population
that is predominantly Black and brown—a phenomenon known
as prison gerrymandering.

On the right, the excesses of the criminal justice system are
more likely to be explained as the result of a permissive culture
and a breakdown of Black families—"moral poverty," to cite a
trope popular in the 1990s—resulting in a surge of crime and a
corresponding rise in public alarm. The War on Drugs and the
ensuing explosion of the prison population, many conservatives
argue, were not acts of racism but responses to legitimate fears.
The conservative backlash has manifested itself most recently
in the attempt by school boards in several states to ban lessons
of American history that dwell on slavery and the slaughter of
Native Americans. The right recoils from depictions of "systemic" racism as unpatriotic. And they contend some of the
proposed remedies—more inclusive school curricula, efforts

80   to diversify hiring and college admissions, the "anti-racist" movement—amount to reverse racism.

Some of her fellow social scientists regard Alexander's indictment of the system as oversimplified. Few are eager to pick a fight with a scholar whose book sold a million copies and helped mobilize a movement for racial justice. And no mainstream social scientist wants to be perceived as dismissing the force of racism in our criminal justice system. But scholars who specialize in studying the relationship between public opinion and government policy prefer a diagnosis that is less conspiratorial—or perhaps less systemic—than Alexander's: crime went up, the electorate got scared, policymakers responded with pitiless sentences, Black men (who, residing in the most crime-afflicted communities, have been perennially overrepresented in the criminal justice system) bore the brunt, and the public for years responded to this cruelty with indifference—because the cruelty was inflicted on Black people. *Not my problem.* This version is more organic than the *New Jim Crow* version, but arguably more damning because it makes society at large complicit, not just in their institutions but in their hearts.

"The motivation for mass incarceration was crime and increased punitiveness," said criminologist Justin Pickett of the State University of New York at Albany. "The reason we were free to get so harsh is, nobody cared about Blacks. Another way to look at it is this: empathy for people being punished really harshly is a brake on policy. It's the thing that keeps you from enacting policies where, for example, people are tortured. But when the mental image of people being hurt by mandatory minimums and three-strike laws and the like is that they're Black, people don't care."

Pickett and others say incendiary politicians and sensation-mongering media, especially local TV if-it-bleeds-it-leads news, contributed to the urge for retribution by making crime more "salient"—that is, more likely to be regarded as an urgent priority.

James Forman Jr., in *Locking Up Our Own*, his Pulitzer Prize–winning 2017 examination of crime and punishment in Black America, points out that Black leaders and their constituents, deeply scarred by the heroin scourge of the 1960s, fervently embraced the War on Drugs. In September 2014, deep into the time of mass incarceration, a Sentencing Project report found 64 percent of Blacks polled (along with 73 percent of whites) said courts treated criminals "not harshly enough."

"How could it be that even after forty years of tough-on-crime tactics, with their attendant toll on black America, 64 percent of African Americans still thought the courts were not harsh enough?" Forman wondered. Part of his answer is what he calls "a central paradox of the African American experience," that Black communities have been simultaneously overpoliced and underpoliced. Many Blacks have long believed that police essentially wrote off Black communities as havens of street crime and drug abuse. Black politicians overcompensated for this neglect with a "politics of responsibility," protecting their own communities by, for example, opposing decriminalization of marijuana use, even though marijuana laws were most severely enforced against Blacks. Likewise, some Black leaders saw mandatory sentences as an equalizer.

Forman, a legal scholar at Yale, stresses that he is not excusing white racism, which "shaped the political, economic and legal context in which the black community and its elected representatives made their choices."

He credits Alexander and like-minded scholars with a "brilliant reframing" of mass incarceration as the foremost civil rights issue of the day, "overwhelmingly the number one issue for law students arriving at my door each fall." But he cautions against treating it as purely about racial injustice. For one thing, that overlooks the opportunity to mobilize the families of white prisoners. Forman recalls going to lobby Connecticut state legislators to reduce the exorbitant prices charged for phone calls from prison. No legislator would say so on the record, but the message was clear that this was a problem for Black and brown people. "A majority of the legislators don't represent those communities," Forman told me. "They don't care."

Especially when crime is rising, Forman added, it's important to couple the outcry over racial injustice with proposals that address public fear, including violence prevention, rehabilitation, and reentry programs.

"The system is racist, *and* . . . It isn't enough to have explained to people that the system is racist. It's important, but, when crime and violence are rising, the *and* becomes front and center on people's minds."

Bruce Western of Columbia, in *Punishment and Inequality in America*, points to another complicating factor. Racial disparities in criminal justice, while enormous, stayed fairly constant during the explosion of imprisonment in the 1980s and 1990s.

What changed most profoundly was the class divide: the lifetime risk of incarceration for men roughly doubled, but nearly all of the added risk fell on men with no more than a high school education, whatever their race.

"Mass incarceration flows along the lines of social and economic inequality," Western told me. "Its signal characteristics are massive racial inequality and massive class inequality. It's a system that concentrates all of its effects on low-income communities of color." That would seem to point to a strategy of addressing racism by addressing poverty.

John Pfaff, a Fordham University law professor and University of Chicago—trained economist, argued in his 2017 book, *Locked In*, that the drug war is "important but unequivocally secondary to other factors." Only 16 percent of those locked up in state prisons, where most prisoners reside, are there for drug crimes, he pointed out. He agrees that mass incarceration is obscene and socially destructive. He believes we could buy greater safety by investing instead in "noncustodial rehabilitation" such as drug treatment, mental health care, and smart probation. But he invites us to rethink our notions about how we got to this state of affairs in the first place, in the hope that doing so will suggest some additional approaches to fixing things. "Most of the reform efforts today," he says, "are looking in the wrong places."

One right place, in Pfaff's view, is the culture of prosecutors, who are rewarded (and reelected) for sending people to prison.

Pfaff notes that, during the 1990s and 2000s, as violent crime and arrests for violent crime both declined, the number of felony cases filed in state courts somehow went up. A lot. "In the

84   end, the probability that a prosecutor would file felony charges against an arrestee basically doubled, and that change pushed prison populations up even as crime dropped," he writes.

Pfaff suggests several explanations for this. There were tens of thousands more prosecutors hired across the country in the 1990s and aughts even after the rising crime of the 1980s had stalled out, and the position of district attorney simultaneously became a more politically powerful one. Prosecutors' discretion, always great, was expanded by courts and legislatures. And public defenders, stuck at comparatively low levels of funding, could not keep up with the caseload.

Pfaff attributes the racial inequity in large part to an imbalance of political power—tough-on-crime prosecutors elected by suburban whites who see the community destruction of mass incarceration from a distance.

Michelle Alexander has held her own in this debate. Raw incarceration data, she told me in an email exchange, misses her point about the War on Drugs. "Some people get so caught up in the prison data . . . that they lose sight of the fact that the drug war was a game-changer culturally and politically. The declaration and escalation of the War on Drugs marked a moment in our history when a group of people defined by race and class was defined as the 'enemy.' A literal war was declared on them, leading to a wave of punitiveness that affected every aspect of our criminal justice system. . . . Counting heads in prisons and jails often obscures that social and political history. It also fails to grasp the significance of the drug war in mobilizing public opinion in support of harsh legislation and policies for all crimes. The drug war corrupted law enforcement by ramping up an us vs. them war mentality, transforming local police into domestic militaries . . . which wound up diverting energy, resources, and attention away from violent crime."

(Pfaff said his differences with Alexander are "mostly semantic." He concurs with her that "the criminal justice system is driven by and exacerbates racial inequality.")

As a theory of how we got to this point, Michelle Alexander supplies a powerful logic, but she offers little comfort to advocates of piecemeal reforms, which she regards as "utterly insufficient." Sure, thanks to advocates of less punitive criminal justice, "Some people who might have spent more than a decade behind bars may spend only a few years. Children who might not otherwise have ever known their parents may have a shot at having relationships with their mother or father, and people may receive additional support—job training or education."

However, she added, "I'm deeply concerned that many people will mistake these reforms for the kind of cultural and institutional transformation that is necessary." The current bipartisan reform consensus, if it survives, might improve a few lives, she conceded, but repairing criminal justice requires "a radical restructuring of our society," potentially driven by "third parties and new political formations" rather than by Republicans or Democrats. She told me, "I'm not enlisting the very people who constructed the system to take charge of now reforming it."

Many students of mass incarceration—including Alexander, whose latest academic home is the Union Theological Seminary—have come to see mass incarceration as fundamentally a moral and spiritual crisis. They say it is not enough to invest in uplifting the poor or to legislate a more even playing field. The country needs a profound reckoning with its original sins, the slaughter of the indigenous population and the

86   enslavement of millions, roughly analogous to Germany's reckoning with the Holocaust.

Amy L. Solomon, a longtime corrections reformer now working in the Biden Justice Department, was struck on a visit to Berlin by the symmetry between Holocaust memorials and a constitution that declares "human dignity shall be inviolable."

"I've spent my career trying to improve incarceration policy and eliminate barriers to successful reentry," she has observed. "But these efforts were largely framed in race-neutral and therefore history-neutral terms. As we reimagine what prisons in America should be, I now see that we must start by acknowledging the oppression, discrimination, and racism that led us to this point and still exist in the system today."

Is that reckoning underway? On the one hand, we have viral videos of Black men killed by cops, Black Lives Matter, a more robust discussion of systemic racism and "anti-racism," and a more honest acknowledgment of our history, such as Bryan Stevenson's campaign to landmark lynching sites, and the *New York Times*'s "1619 Project," focusing on America's founding through the lens of slavery. On the other hand, we have a spike in violent crime, a right-wing backlash against any curriculum that smacks of blaming white America, voter suppression in red states, a Senate that serves as a tank trap for legislation aimed at social justice, and the short attention spans of American voters.

College Behind Bars

After the 1994 crime bill cut off federal Pell grants for incarcerated students, the number of college programs in American correctional facilities plummeted from nearly 800 to fewer than a dozen. One of the few surviving programs was at San Quentin, California's oldest state prison, which, when the crime bill was signed, had been negotiating with nearby Patten University to teach a few college-degree courses at the prison. Founded in the forties as the Oakland Bible Institute, Patten mainly served aspiring Evangelical ministers, but it was accredited by the Western Association of Schools and Colleges. So when Congress cut off the Pell funding, Patten and the prison decided to go ahead anyway, using volunteer teachers and textbooks donated by publishers. Later, when Patten was acquired by an online startup, San Quentin's educators incorporated as an independent college, naming it Mount Tamalpais for the mountain that looms over the bayside prison complex. It was the first independent liberal arts institution where a felony conviction was the price of admission.

88   Because San Quentin is embedded in affluent, liberal Marin County, and because it has had some unusually progressive wardens, it has grown rich in programming for its residents. When I visited in 2016, the prison had 3,000 volunteers donating their time to an incarcerated population of about 3,700. The men can sign up for therapeutic services like anger management and substance abuse counseling, for yoga and meditation, and for trades like plumbing and electronics. There is a Silicon Valley computer coding program that pays prisoners to perform contract work and prepares students for employment when they get out. San Quentin residents produce a serious newspaper, the *San Quentin News*, and an excellent podcast on prison life, called *Ear Hustle*.

But the heart of San Quentin's rehabilitation culture is Mount Tamalpais College. The catalogue for the associate degree program lists about ninety courses, the whole gamut of sciences and humanities, taught by a volunteer faculty of professors and grad students from Bay Area campuses.

"Like I told my father," one resident joked when I visited, "this is like a men's liberal arts college, except there's less violence and less drinking."

In 2018, researchers at the Rand Corporation surveyed thirty-seven years of American prison studies and concluded that, on average, prisoners who take part in educational programming—including everything from basic literacy to post-secondary—are 28 percent less likely to be returned to captivity. Other studies suggest that the higher an incarcerated student progresses up the academic ladder, the less likely she is to "recidivate."

Jody Lewen, who has overseen San Quentin's academic offerings for more than twenty years, objects to the emphasis

on recidivism and favors other ways to measure the impact of
in-prison higher education, including academic and professional attainment, social and psychological development, civic
engagement, and health and wellness. "Recidivism is an abom-
inably low standard to use in measuring an educational program," she told me. "Stanford would never say, 'We know we are
providing a quality education because our students are almost
never sent to prison.'"

Before she encountered San Quentin, Lewen had an "almost
cultlike" devotion to academia. She grew up on the Upper West
Side of Manhattan, the daughter of a social worker (later a psy-
choanalyst) and a patent attorney (later an intellectual prop-
erty lawyer). A graduate of prestigious schools (Horace Mann
preparatory school and Wesleyan University), she spent her
post-grad years in Germany, acquiring an MA in comparative
literature and philosophy, then moved to another bastion of
abstract thought, the University of California Berkeley Rhetoric
Department, to work on her PhD. (Her dissertation topic was
*On the Role of Images of Matter and Space in Psychic Life, Litera-
ture, and Psychoanalysis.*)

At a conference on psychoanalysis, she overheard someone
talking about the San Quentin program, volunteered to co-teach
a communications class at the prison, and had an intoxicating
encounter with "actual life."

"In academia, you kind of know that everybody you're going
to serve is already going to be fine," she told me. At San Quentin
she felt she was influencing lives that were not at all assured
of being fine. When she veered from the traditional academic
career path to join the San Quentin project full-time, her faculty advisors were astonished. They encouraged her to do it as

90   a hobby. They told her that instead of a tenured paycheck she'd be begging donors for her own salary ("which turned out to be true"). But, most disheartening, they didn't seem to see the value in teaching a population so far off the beaten career track.

"Here I was, in the year 2000, being cautioned—in large part by intellectuals—against devoting my actual life to confronting a dire humanitarian crisis: that of the US prison system," she said. "Better to stay on a conventional college campus and read Foucault than traipse up and down the tiers of an actual cell block. Safer to sit in an armchair reading Hannah Arendt on the banality of evil, than to engage face-to-face with a massive and brutal bureaucracy that is grinding up the lives of hundreds of thousands of human beings as we speak."

Twenty years of running a college behind bars has made her a tough-love critic of higher education. She sees too many academics who devalue the hard craft of teaching in favor of theoretical research, who confuse privilege with intellectual potential, who bring "elitist" attitudes to the prison classroom.

At Mount Tamalpais, admission is open to any prisoner with a high school diploma or a GED equivalent, first come, first served. Even when they meet that basic requirement, few of the applicants are ready for college courses. Lewen estimates that a third of the teaching workload consists of remedial courses and college prep. She regards this egalitarian ethic as a "transfer of social capital"—of power—to some of society's most margin-alized members, and she is a little scornful of college-in-prison programs that cherry-pick the most promising students and pass over the victims of educational neglect. "Getting stu-dents ready to go to college is actually a more radical and more demanding and more complex endeavor than getting the college degree itself," she told me.

Lewen raises an annual budget, now about $4 million, without state or federal money. She welcomes the return of Pell grants, but worries that some colleges will treat incarcerated students as a profit center, without holding them to the same standards—or investing the same resources—as on-campus students. Some colleges, for example, don't offer imprisoned students a coherent academic program—where advanced calculus builds on intermediate calculus, etc.—but just random courses depending on what teachers are available that semester. "I would say there's a tremendous amount that's really mediocre," she told me, and the scramble for Pell money could make things worse.

"Pell is like pouring blood into the ocean and watching what the sharks do," Lewen said.

Across the country in New York, Max Kenner, founder and director of the Bard Prison Initiative, shares Lewen's worry about mediocrity in prison college programs.

Bard operates in six New York prisons and advises a consortium of colleges and universities around the country that offer degrees to incarcerated students.

"We work hard to create an experience that resembles, as closely as possible, what happens on campus," he told me, "but we are up against a bigotry of expectations. Educators show up at the prison and are astounded by a level of academic performance that would be considered mediocre anywhere else. It leads to a lack of seriousness, a lack of ambition, and a sort of detour around what can be truly transformative in college in prison."

92   Admission to Bard's programs is more selective than San
Quentin's. Applicants are gathered in a classroom, handed two
or three short readings—a poem, an op-ed, the opening pas-
sage of a novel—and given a couple of hours to respond. Several
faculty members read the resulting work, and the most promising candidates are called back for intensive interviews. "We're
looking for a combination of preparedness, potential, and inspi-
ration," Kenner told me.

Kenner and Lewen have a running argument about which
prisoners should be admitted to their programs. But as Kenner
points out, this is essentially an argument over a principle,
because in real life neither program comes close to meeting the
need. Even San Quentin's more inclusive program leaves out
most of the roughly 70 percent of prison residents who never
finished high school.

"Both Jody and I fill every seat we can," he said.

Kelsey Kauffman came earlier than Jody Lewen to her disen-
chantment with academia and her enthusiasm for "actual life."
As a teenager, she dropped out of college three times—the third
time to live for five months with a remote tribe of active headhunters in the Philippines. Her father, Rear Admiral Draper L.
Kauffman, had a storied career as a demolitions expert, godfa-
ther of the Navy Seals, and superintendent of the Naval Academy,
where he aggressively recruited and mentored students of color,
some of whom rose to become among the Navy's first Black flag
officers. In 1969, when she was studying the headhunters, Yale
opened enrollment to women; Kauffman applied "as a joke,"
mainly to show some dubious Yalie relatives that she could get
in, and when she was accepted felt she should probably go. She

found it excruciatingly boring and shamelessly misogynistic.
There was, for starters, the anthropology teacher whose intro-
ductory class featured a slide show of close-ups of women's
breasts, in which he professed to find insights into different civ-
ilizations. (Kauffman never took another anthro course.) "The
headhunters were much more educational than Yale."

The summer after her graduation in 1971, the Attica Prison
bloodbath gripped her interest. She could only think of two ways
to satisfy her curiosity about the mysteries of prison, and sticking
up a liquor store was not her style, so she took a job as a corrections officer at the York Correctional Institution, a women's
prison in the Connecticut village of Niantic. (It's now the site of
the experimental WORTH unit described in chapter five.) It was
an easygoing place in the early 1970s: 125 women, many of them
sent away for alleged promiscuity (the offense, on the books until
1971, was formally known as being in "manifest danger of falling
into habits of vice.") The staff and residents shared family-style
meals on holidays, and tended strawberry plants in the garden.
Kauffman was assigned to an experimental unit run by Harvard
University psychologist Lawrence Kohlberg, where the inmates
were given a voice in major decisions in the belief this would
exert a positive influence on their moral maturity.

Kauffman overcame her distaste for academia long enough
to enroll in a graduate program at Harvard, where, for her doctoral dissertation, she researched the lives of prison officers at
four facilities in Massachusetts, including the famously menacing maximum security prison at Walpole. She turned her
thesis into a book, *Prison Officers and Their World*, published in
1988, which portrays the guardians and the guarded as fellow
victims of a failed system.

94   In 1997, Kauffman was intrigued by a local news item in Indiana, where her husband had taken a professorship at DePauw University. The story told of two whistleblowers fired by the state corrections department for exposing a network of white supremacists, called the Brotherhood, working within the state's prison system. Kauffman teamed up with the whistleblowers, mobilized local ministers, mastered the tools of the Freedom of Information Act, and produced a damning exposé that toppled the commissioner of corrections.

When Pell grants ended in 1994, Indiana was one of a few states that stepped in with state money to keep college programs afloat. But in 2011, without debate, the state legislature cut off that funding. "College programs in all but one of the state's prisons collapsed almost overnight as colleges and universities—public and private—withdrew not only their instructors but also their books, computers, and supplies," Kauffman recalled. The following year, Kauffman and some friends got state approval to restart the college program in the maximum security Indiana Women's Prison, using all volunteers.

Kauffman built a model of prison education very different from San Quentin and Bard. Along with the usual courses in math and history, taught mostly by retired professors from central Indiana universities, Kauffman created an advanced course in public policy that might be called rehabilitation by civic combat.

As my Marshall Project colleague Eli Hager reported:

The class of about a dozen women studied civic literacy— how to write policy proposals, contact elected representatives, and talk to the media. Every session, they pored

over the fine print of bills then under consideration by the
Indiana state legislature, especially those related to incarceration, drug addiction, domestic violence, and sexual
assault, the issues they knew best. They held mock committee meetings and looked for clauses they thought could
be amended.

In one instance, they invited women state legislators to
watch as they poured water on the cheap, nonabsorbent men-
strual pads stocked at the prison; the lawmakers reported the
problem to the lieutenant governor and she called corrections
officials on the carpet.

With Kauffman's guidance, a group of women won legisla-
tive approval for a plan, called Constructing Our Future, to help
the city deal with a plague of abandoned houses in East Indianapolis. Women in their final year before parole would be given
work release to learn construction skills. Upon completing
their sentences they would each put in 5,000 hours of sweat
equity renovating the derelict homes, and be rewarded with a
home. The students would graduate from prison with employable skills and a place to live, two of the essential prerequisites
for a chance at normal lives. Although changes in leadership in
the Indiana Department of Correction and the pandemic have
thus far prevented the full realization of the program inside
the prison, former students who have left IWP now lead Constructing Our Future outside. They opened their first home in
2021.

Meanwhile, IWP's history students delved into the prison
archives and uncovered the story of a network of Catholic
prisons commonly known as Magdalene Laundries where,

96   beginning in the 1840s, women were sentenced to hard labor for prostitution and other sex offenses. The students' work has been expanded into a book to be published by New Press.

Kauffman's students accomplished all this without a major philanthropic sponsor, a Scandinavian guidebook, or the consistent backing of the state's political hierarchy. What worked in Indiana was a management style that let good ideas bubble up from the students and held the promise of tangible outcomes (published history, construction skills, influence in the legislature). Kauffman's experience as a prison officer and her empathetic book on their work undoubtedly bought her credibility with the prison staff, who facilitated her program rather than obstructing it. She would add that her shoestring budget—$5,000, compared to $4 million at Mount Tamalpais and $10 million at Bard—was in some ways a blessing in disguise, attracting teachers who were committed to the work, sparing her the distraction of endless fundraising and rendering the program less vulnerable to budget cuts and political whims. (Pell today, gone tomorrow.)

As different as their programs are in scale, resources, and approach, Lewen, Kauffman, and Kenner—and all of the best college-in-prison educators I have met—share a conviction that their work is not just an act of kindness or even an investment in public safety, but a kind of reparations.

The Afterlife

When you leave prison in Texas, you get a $50 check, a bus ticket, and a kind of vertigo. After decades in which you have never had to choose what's for dinner, never worked an ATM, let alone Venmo, never so much as opened a door for yourself, you face a dizzying onslaught of choices and obligations, baffling devices and unfamiliar customs, and temptations.

Bryan Kelley, who made parole after almost twenty-two years of a life sentence for murder, calls these encounters "welcome-to-freedom moments." Here's one of his: The day he emerged from behind the red brick walls of the state prison in Huntsville, his mom, cousins, and friends were there to meet him. After hugs and tears, they all packed into a rented Chevy Suburban to head for Dallas. "About two blocks down the road," Kelley recalled, "I looked up and every single person, including my five-year-old cousin, was on their phone and totally ignoring me." Welcome to freedom.

Kelley was exceptionally fortunate. Not only did he have supportive family, he was a graduate of the nonprofit Prison

98 Entrepreneurship Program, which grooms prisoners from sixty Texas prisons in the skills and attitudes necessary to start a business, or at least to find a secure foothold in an existing business. Kelley is now the chief executive officer of the program.

Of the few dozen men released from Huntsville in his cohort, Kelly reckons 80 percent had no one waiting outside the walls. They used their tickets to get to the Houston or Dallas bus terminals, where merchants of every conceivable vice waited to relieve them of their $50 allowance.

"It's like darkness welcomes men home from prison with wide open arms," Kelley said.

As Reuben Jonathan Miller writes in *Halfway Home*, his vivid account of what he learned as a chaplain to the incarcerated and, later, as a sociologist, "mass incarceration has an afterlife, and that afterlife is a supervised society—a hidden social world and an alternate legal reality. The prison lives on through the people who've been convicted long after they complete their sentences, and it lives on through the grandmothers, lovers, and children forced to share their burdens because they are never really allowed to pay their so-called debt to society."

Parole (granted by a board after some time served) and probation (assigned by a judge as part of the original sentence) are for most prisoners the first stage of the afterlife. They get less attention than incarceration, but parole and probation regulate the lives of 4.5 million Americans, more than twice as many as are confined in prisons and jails. Because a parolee can be returned to prison for technical infractions such as missed appointments or traces of drugs in a urine sample, the supervised society is a precarious place. That has never been more true than during the pandemic, when the stress of finding safe

shelter—and the lure of escape into drugs and alcohol—were
compounded.

Martin Horn, a former New York State parole director and now a professor at the John Jay College of Criminal Justice, has long argued for a radical rethinking of post-prison supervision. "I used to say if we furloughed all of my parole officers in New York State for three months, who would notice the difference?" Horn told me. "We don't make it safer or improve the lives of the people under supervision. The only thing we're interested in when we release a person from prison is that they don't commit a new crime. How they accomplish that is really their business."

Horn has suggested giving parolees vouchers they could use to buy education, housing, drug treatment, or other services and let them decide what help they need to reenter society. These are services the current bureaucracy performs poorly, if at all. Horn concedes that to prepare prisoners for such an independent life would require transforming prisons into prep schools, devoted to graduating people with marketable skills and control of their demons.

A somewhat less radical option, already practiced in New York City for parolees regarded as low-risk, is to replace parole officers with ATM-like kiosks that scan fingerprints. Check in once a month, answer a few questions on a computer screen, and get on with your life. Alternatively, Vincent Schiraldi, a longtime reformer—most recently New York City's commissioner of corrections—has suggested simply outsourcing supervision to nongovernmental organizations that would be paid to help the formerly incarcerated navigate the outside world.

The most respected reentry programs tend to be nonprofits financed by donors, staffed largely by volunteers, and led by

100   charismatic figures—often, like Bryan Kelley, leaders shaped by their own intimate experience of the prison world.

For Elizabeth Gaynes, president of the New York–based Osborne Association, that experience was being married to prison. Her husband was a Black activist, Jomo Davis, who spent most of their marriage in prison or on the run. "My children's dad—first he was underground on the FBI's most wanted list, and then he was in prison for twenty-five years," Gaynes said. Though the couple separated, he kept up a correspondence from prison with their daughter Emani, read the books she was assigned in school, and when he was released in 2009—frail and slipping into dementia—Emani became his caregiver. (Davis died in 2018.) Not surprisingly, parenting classes and family visitation are central components of the Osborne reentry repertoire, along with job training, mental health, and substance abuse counseling. In 2015, the state gave Osborne control of an abandoned prison, the Fulton Correctional Facility, which is being renovated as a 135-bed transitional residence for released prisoners, especially the elderly and infirm.

Like most of the best reentry programs, Osborne begins its work well before release and continues to offer help long after for those who want it. Like most of the best reentry programs, it does not begin to meet the need. One hundred thirty-five beds, Gaynes notes, is "a drop in the bucket." New York paroles around 4,000 people in a typical year.

Bryan Kelley was raised in small-town Kansas, in a family of alcoholics and addicts, and surrendered young to the thrall of cocaine. He killed a man in a drug deal gone bad, and in 1992 was sentenced to life in prison, where he took belated control of his life—reconnecting with his faith, earning a degree in psychology, and volunteering as a mentor. On his thirteenth bid for parole he won approval—then requested that his release be postponed a year so he could complete his studies with the Prison Entrepreneurship Program.

Kelley has a shaved head and the earnest patter of a motivational speaker. PEP is open to inmates who are within three years of parole, have a clean disciplinary record, and convince recruiters that they genuinely want to change.

"What we're looking for," Kelley told me, "is not educational achievement, it's not previous business knowledge. It's really just someone who is sick and tired of being sick and tired, and is moldable and coachable and willing to do the hard work of change. . . . It's not aptitude, it's attitude." While PEP accepts students of all faiths, its "ten driving values" are "rooted in scripture" and 80 percent of its volunteers identify as Christian, Kelley told me.

Those who enter the program are transferred to a separate prison unit where a volunteer corps of coaches and business executives teaches a "mini-MBA" program that entails developing and pitching a business plan, alongside classes in accounting and public speaking and basic life skills. Upon release they are offered lodging in one of PEP's halfway houses, assigned a case manager to help walk them through the logistics of freedom, and plugged into a network of potential employers. More than 2,800 men have graduated since the program was founded in 2004, and the results are impressive. Almost all of them are employed, mostly in service industries like trucking, landscaping, and construction. Three years after completing the program, according to studies by two outside reviewers, only

8 percent end up back in prison, compared with a Texas-wide return rate of 23 percent. About one in five own their own businesses. More than 40 percent own their homes. Of course, PEP only accepts the prisoners most likely to succeed, but success is success, and for those leaving prisons success is too scarce.

Scarce, in part, because a society that celebrates reinvention and professes to believe in second chances has assured that a criminal's debt to society is rarely marked "paid in full." By one estimate, the lives of the formerly incarcerated are governed by 45,000 federal and state laws.

They include the loss of established rights, such as the rights to vote or own a gun; limits on personal freedom, such as curfews, travel restrictions, or, for the undocumented, deportation; dissemination of damaging information, such as public sex offender registries; and loss of opportunities and benefits, such as school admission, eligibility for subsidized housing, licenses for various occupations, and small business loans.

Even a well-established, business-friendly, Christianity-infused program like PEP faces an array of regulatory impediments that complicate the afterlife. "Most people don't want ex-felons coming into their homes to repair things, so it's much easier [for a new plumber or electrician] to get into commercial trades than residential," Kelley said. An advocacy group called the Collateral Consequences Resource Center grades states based on their restoration of rights of the formerly incarcerated. Texas ranks forty-eighth.

And those are just the formal legal impediments. Most people who have done time in prison have faced some measure of suspicion, discrimination, or ostracism. It's a de facto double

jeopardy, piling society's punishment on top of the one handed
down in court.

One of the most gifted alumni of the Indiana Women's Prison is
Michelle Jones, whose story my Marshall Project colleague Eli
Hager reported in 2017 on the front page of the *New York Times*.

"In a breathtaking feat of rehabilitation," he wrote, "Jones,
now forty-five, became a published scholar of American history while behind bars, and presented her work by videoconfer-
ence to historians' conclaves and the Indiana General Assembly.
With no internet access and a prison library that skewed toward
romance novels, she led a team of inmates that pored through
reams of photocopied documents from the state archives to
produce the Indiana Historical Society's best research project
last year," that being the story of the Catholic women's prisons
known as Magdalene Laundries.

"As prisoner No. 970554, Ms. Jones also wrote several
dance compositions and historical plays, one of which is slated
to open at an Indianapolis theater in December."

All this while serving twenty years of a fifty-year sentence
for murder.

Granted early release, Jones was accepted into Harvard's
prestigious graduate history program, one of eighteen students
selected from more than three hundred applicants.

But then, as if to prove that our faith in redemption is limited even at an ostensible citadel of progressivism, the university withdrew its offer.

Jones's critics offered a variety of explanations for the
unusual reversal.

One was a complaint that Jones was not sufficiently forth-coming in her application. An unsolicited, three-paragraph addendum she submitted on the subject of her crime was less a confession than an outpouring of her own pain. "My inability to psychologically cope with my own abandonment, sudden parenthood, and an abusive husband led to a complete emotional and mental breakdown on my part," she wrote. "I left my son alone in our home and he died." Now, she added, "My son, Brandon, is gone, and I have spent the last twenty years engaged in living a life that is redemptive, a life that he could be proud of, because he is not here to live his own life." Some faculty readers contended that this account minimized her crime "to the point of misrepresentation."

Another professed concern, patronizing if not downright laughable, was that after twenty years behind bars Jones would be intimidated by such an elite pressure cooker as Harvard.

But at the heart of Harvard's rejection was the crime itself, and what right-wing critics might do with it: Jones left her four-year-old son alone to die, then disposed of the body, which was never found. One of the professors who challenged her admission explained that "frankly, we knew that anyone could just punch her crime into Google, and Fox News would probably say that PC-liberal Harvard gave two hundred grand of funding to a child murderer, who also happened to be a minority." (Jones is Black.) "I mean, c'mon."

After Jones's story emerged, scores of faculty signed letters castigating the school's leaders for betraying Harvard's liberal values. The prosecutor in the murder case—while rejecting the word "redemption"—said Jones had paid her debt and that Harvard was effectively resentencing her. More than 1,100 readers

wrote to the *Times*, debating whether some crimes were unfor-
givable, some offenders beyond rehabilitation.

"Abusing and killing a young child is not washed away by twenty years in prison; it is, and rightly should be, a burden carried for life," wrote one reader.

"How much is too much to be forgiven for?" countered another. "If we can't forgive, what is the point of trying to rehabilitate?"

Jones landed on her feet, as a doctoral student in American studies at New York University, and subsequently won several fellowships, including a 2017–18 research fellowship at the Charles Warren Center for Studies in American History—at Harvard.

Her choice of a subject for graduate study seemed foreordained: the stigma of prison.

"The afterlife for the formerly incarcerated is one of ongoing punishment and unending payment," she wrote in a paper drawing on interviews with the formerly incarcerated and published by the University of Hawaii. "Conviction for a crime requires repeated and extensive biographic disclosure in interviews with parole/probation officers, doctors, employment agents, loan officers, and leasing agents, beyond the local need for information related to the task at hand."

She went on to argue that people who have paid for their crimes are entitled to fashion their own "narrative," including "dissembling." Without explicitly asserting a right to lie, she endorsed "selective disclosure" and presenting a false front. Jones argued that "dissemblance allows the newly released to carve out mental space to reenter society on our own terms and gather resources to avoid reincarceration. In order to face a

106   hostile world that routinely disregards, violates, and discrimi-
nates, the formerly incarcerated present a dissembling face." In
the time before emancipation this was "a strategy that enslaved
African American women (and men) used to survive and resist
their captivity and avoid sexual violence. In effect, they showed
one face to the master while they raised their children and
taught them survival strategies."

Dissembling is not a strategy generally endorsed by journalists or historians—occupations that profess a reverence for
unfettered truth—but I expect Jones's argument would find
considerable sympathy in our post-privacy world. A criminal record has always been a handicap to some degree, but the
internet has made it immeasurably easier to find out just about
anything about just about anyone. The more sensational the
information, the more likely it is that an algorithm will cough it
up in your search results. The ubiquity of Google has also given
birth to a cottage industry of scam artists who promise, for a
price, to purge your record and mug shot from the cyber-record.

The past decade has also seen an unlikely coalition mobilized to lower some of the barriers faced by people with criminal records. It includes business groups defending would-be
employees and entrepreneurs, libertarian conservatives, the
ACLU, and faith-based organizations. They have had some success in courts and legislatures. The Collateral Consequences
Resource Center, which monitors and advocates restoration of
rights, counts 151 laws passed by states in 2021. These include
measures making it easier to seal or expunge criminal records,
especially for juveniles and low-level drug convictions; ending
discrimination in the issuing of occupational licenses; banning
discrimination in housing; and restoring voting and gun rights.

"Collateral consequences should be tailored to the crime, and limited," said Margaret Love, executive director of the center, which she helped create in 2014. "Certainly you want to keep guns out of the hands of people who would use them in a dangerous manner. If you commit a big fraud people ought to know, to be wary of you in the financial markets. But there ought to be a way to get past that and redeem yourself."

Love was the US Pardon Attorney in the 1990s, reviewing cases for presidential clemency, and her practice specializes in clemency and restoration of rights.

Another effort aimed at diminishing the stigma of prison is the "ban the box" campaign, which calls for eliminating questions about an applicant's criminal record in the first round of applying for a job or school admissions. The federal government, 37 states, and more than 150 cities and counties have dropped the question of criminal history in the first stage of filling public jobs, as has the Common App widely used in college admissions. "Banning the box" does not prohibit criminal background checks after an applicant has a foot in the door. And there is some evidence that these well-intentioned efforts may lead employers, forbidden to ask about criminal history, to use racial profiling instead.

In my own business, the past few years have seen a lively debate about the way we cover people enmeshed in the criminal justice system. At their worst, news media have been accomplices in the vilification, dwelling on the lurid details of crimes, featuring perp walks and menacing mug shots of the accused, attaching labels that amount to a scarlet letter. But even news organizations that resist the temptation to sensationalize are protective of their right to public records and free speech.

The European Union recognizes a so-called "right to be for-gotten" that requires online news organizations to purge old arrest records from their system under some circumstances. Press freedom organizations have fended off claims of a sim-ilar right in the US—notably in a 2015 court ruling against a woman who sued the Hearst Corporation for refusing to take down an accurate report of her marijuana arrest after her record was expunged.

This country's ultimate pariahs, in prison and in the afterlife, are sex offenders, who are commonly required to have their crimes disclosed on public registries, and are banished from living in proximity to places where children gather.

America was the first country to require sex-crime regis-tries. (The federal statute, commonly referred to as Megan's Law, was part of the punitive 1994 crime bill.) Another eigh-teen countries have followed, though in most of them the reg-istries are accessible only to law enforcement. The usual justification—apart from the visceral repugnance of the crime—is a belief that those who commit sex crimes are highly likely to be repeat offenders. As the *New York Times*'s Adam Liptak explained in 2017, the notion that sex-offender recid-ivism is "frightening and high" has been embraced by the Supreme Court but called into question by extensive research. Burglars, robbers, and drug offenders are twice as likely as sex offenders to be re-arrested after release from prison. A metic-ulous meta-study commissioned by the Canadian Department of Public Safety—taking into account the caveats that sexual crimes are underreported and that there is a wide disparity of views about what constitutes sexual assault—found that most sex offenders do not commit new sex crimes. Noting that some categories of offender (molesters of boys, for example) are far more likely to commit new sex crimes, the authors concluded that "blanket policies that treat all sexual offenders as 'high risk' waste resources by oversupervising lower risk offenders and risk diverting resources from the truly high-risk offenders who could benefit from increased supervision and human service."

Policymakers rarely make such fine distinctions.

Emily Kassie and Beth Schwartzapfel of the Marshall Project explored the outcast lives of one group of registered sex offenders in Miami-Dade County, Florida, who became homeless nomads, banished by a confluence of federal, state, and local laws.

> The feds say they're not allowed in public housing. The state says they can't live within 1,000 feet of a day care center, park, playground, or school. The county says they can't live within 2,500 feet of a school. In a place so densely populated, forbidden zones are everywhere. And in the narrow slivers of permitted space, affordable apartments with open-minded landlords are nearly impossible to come by.

Many of the wandering outcasts are also on probation, which comes with its own requirements, including a curfew and an ankle bracelet and GPS device that has to be charged every day, to transmit their movements to a probation officer.

> Failure to register is a felony. Registering at one address and staying at another is a felony. Failure to report a new

110   email address, tattoo, car, boat, or job is a felony. And an
           offender on probation who isn't in place during curfew, or
           who doesn't charge his GPS box, or misses appointments
           or breaks any of dozens of other rules, could end up back in
           prison for years.

           The nomads' crimes ranged from downloading child porn
           to violent assault. There was a former teacher who molested
           students in his care, and a man who raped his stepdaughter
           over four years starting when she was twelve. "It's easy to see
           why lawmakers would want to banish these men to the far-
           thest reaches of society," Kassie and Schwartzapfel wrote. "But
           beyond the moral arguments about where sex offenders should
           live are the practical considerations of being human: They need
           to eat and sleep. They need a little money to get by. They need
           somewhere to pass the hours. And so they begin and end each
           day with a question: How do you build a life in the shadows of a
           society that no longer wants you?"

A World Apart

"The American prison system was built with men in mind," Keri Blakinger has written. "The uniforms are made to fit male bodies. About 70 percent of the guards are men. The rules are made to control male social structures and male violence." Before being paroled and reinventing herself as a journalist specializing in criminal justice, Blakinger spent nearly two years in New York lockups on drug charges.

The disproportionate attention paid to men is understandable: women make up only about 10 percent of those confined in prisons and jails, although their population has been growing twice as fast as men's, partly due to the proliferation of opioid abuse. Women's prisons constitute a small, comparatively peaceful island in the archipelago of incarceration. Men's prisons are more confrontational, more tribal, more volatile. Men define the most obvious problems of prison, and so they tend to define the ostensible solutions—including both the paramilitary culture and the opportunities for rehabilitation. Women's needs, from the prosaic (an adequate supply of

112   tampons) to the profound (contact with their children), often get short shrift.

The visiting room of a male prison usually attracts loyal wives and girlfriends, who regularly travel hours on a bus, bringing children, depositing money in commissary accounts, and sometimes bearing contraband drugs or cell phones. In the visiting rooms of women's prisons, husbands and boyfriends are more often MIA.

So women turn to one another.

What most Americans know of women's prisons probably comes from the Netflix version of *Orange Is the New Black*, based on Piper Kerman's memoir of her year in prison. Women who have done time tend to find that the show lapses into caricature, dwells on the prurient, and doesn't capture the grinding tedium and daily humiliation women face in prison. It's TV, after all.

One important thing the show gets right, though, is the way incarcerated women organize themselves for survival.

Unlike men, who tend to cluster along racial and gang lines, "what women tend to do is re-create family structures in prison," said Vivian Nixon, a formerly imprisoned activist who recently retired as executive director of the College and Community Fellowship, which helps women make the transition from prison to higher education. "They have meals together. They do rec time together. They study together. They sign up for the same activities. It's a much more communal environment. And lifelong friendships are formed in women's prisons. I'm still close to people I was incarcerated with in 1997."

Sometimes—more commonly than in male prisons, where homophobia is rife—the bonds are romantic or sexual.

"Everyone has a prison girlfriend," Keri Blakinger told me. "Sometimes it just means you're holding hands in the rec yard. You're just sort of glorified best friends. But sometimes it means you're fucking under the bunk when the CO leaves." Prison couples are often, as the saying goes, "gay for the stay, straight at the gate." But sometimes couples get out and remain together for years.

Prison families are sources of emotional support in a world where guards are often abusive (female officers as well as their male counterparts) and the men in their outside lives have disappeared.

In her 2005 portrayal of life in a Massachusetts women's prison, *A World Apart*, Cristina Rathbone says that in male prisons the authorities worry about violence, but in women's prisons they worry about intimacy. This is not to suggest that women's prisons are free of violence or that men in prison never form close relationships. But the communal culture in women's prisons can be taken by authorities as a kind of defiance, a challenge to order.

The women's quasi-familial bonds are also a point of vulnerability and thus a source of control. "You can get a ticket for giving your friend a back rub or hugging too close," Blakinger said. "The degree to which you're expected to not touch another human being for years is not realistic or healthy or normal. In my day, sitting on your best friend's bed could get you put in solitary."

Jennifer Toon, who spent nineteen years in Texas prisons for murder, said the threat of being separated was powerful leverage.

"It was a very big deal on a woman's unit: 'I don't want to get moved,'" she said. "Men don't care if they have to go to seg [segregated confinement] to stand up for their rights. But it's hard to get women to protest anything or stand together if getting in trouble means I'm going to get moved away from this group of people that's like a family to me."

Women who have done time say that correctional officers are obsessed with lesbianism and spend an inordinate amount of time patrolling for evidence of illicit sexual contact—whether because it is a breach of discipline or out of more voyeuristic interest is not always clear.

"They tell you it's a safety issue," said Stephanie Covington, a clinical psychologist and consultant on treatment of addiction and trauma in prison. "Women form very strong emotional attachments, and if they break up, what you have is women who are crying, distressed, sometimes there's some aggressive behavior. What mostly happens is just lots of tears, but the criminal justice system can't deal with feelings, whether it's rage or grief."

That's not to minimize the very real incidence of sexual violence in prisons and jails—a danger for men but a greater danger for women. Female prisoners are subjected to rape and other sexual assault, sexual extortion, and groping during body searches. Male correctional officials watch women undressing, in the shower, or on the toilet. Although reporting of sexual violence has improved since Congress passed the (wishfully named) Prison Rape Elimination Act of 2003, filing a complaint still entails a risk of retaliation. In many states prison officers have access to inmates' personal files, including their complaints, and there are abundant tools of intimidation beyond physical reprisals, from limiting child visitation to solitary confinement to issuing misconduct tickets that can jeopardize parole.

A 2008 government survey of nearly 18,000 former inmates, presumably somewhat less vulnerable to reprisals than those still inside, found 8.7 percent of men and 16.1 percent of women reported having been "sexually victimized" during their most recent incarceration. That includes "all types of unwanted sexual activity with other inmates (e.g., oral, anal, or vaginal penetration, hand jobs, or touching of the inmate's buttocks, thighs, penis, breasts, or vagina in a sexual way), abusive sexual contacts with other inmates, and both willing and unwilling sexual activity with staff," which is illegal even if not coerced.

The Believe Women movement apparently has not yet penetrated the corrections system. The Bureau of Justice Statistics' most recent analysis of data from adult prisons and jails, covering 2016 to 2018, found that, of alleged inmate-on-inmate sexual offenses, one in thirteen was considered "substantiated." For allegations against staff, the number was only one in twenty.

(Incarceration is even more of a sexual horror show for the tiny population of imprisoned transgender people. According to a 2015 survey by the National Center for Transgender Equality, they are ten times as likely as the general prison population to be sexually assaulted by their fellow inmates and five times as likely to be sexually assaulted by staff. Transgender prisoners also face other challenges behind bars, including denials of medical care and lengthy stays in solitary confinement.)

With some notable exceptions, women's prisons offer fewer rehabilitation programs, and they often fit a gender stereotype—cosmetology but not business administration or operating a forklift. Morgan Godvin, who did two years in FCI

116　　Dublin, a federal correctional institution for women near Oakland, California, said rehabilitation was scarce and half-hearted.

"There was zero opportunity for college credit," she said. "Even the GED program was a joke. I did RDAP, the residential drug and alcohol program. A complete joke. Often they would just put on a movie and give us some make-work activity. They put on *Batman* and they're like, 'Identify a thinking error in the Joker's character.'"

Incarcerated people, men and women, arrive wearing scars of physical and emotional abuse, but women's wounds are different. They are far more likely to report suffering sexual violence in childhood, more likely to have suffered at the hands of people expected to love them, and they are more likely to have had the abuse continue into adolescence and adulthood.

According to criminologist Nena Messina, who has done extensive study in California prisons, corrections officials are loath to spend state money on dealing with women's trauma in prison or post-release.

"They're saying, 'we'll deal with addiction,'" she said, "'we'll deal with anger, we'll deal with criminal thinking. We'll provide programs that have those flag words in them. But we won't talk about trauma,'" for fear of the volcanic emotions that might be released. Nonprofit groups have shown considerable success alleviating depression, anxiety, and PTSD in California's three women's prisons, often by training inmates serving life sentences to run small, supportive group sessions. But officials say they focus behavioral programming on prisoners most at risk of returning to crime—men. That's pretty much standard practice in American prisons, but it has a perverse effect: women are punished for having lower rates of recidivism.

Messina, who speaks with the exasperation of someone who has been shouting into the wind for twenty years, challenges the prevailing wisdom in corrections—the risk-need-responsivity model, discussed in chapter two, which says the highest priority should be the most dangerous offenders and the focus should be on factors that change criminal behavior. The problem is, those factors are different for women.

"Compared with their male counterparts, justice-involved women have different pathways into, and out of, crime and addiction," Messina said. "They respond to supervision and custody differently, and they have a higher prevalence of lifelong trauma and abuse, co-occurring mental health issues, and other complex interpersonal and financial disadvantages."

Risk factors that are more prevalent among women include intimate partner violence, involvement with child protective services, adolescent pregnancy, prostitution, homelessness, and dependency on others for financial support.

"It's not just that women are short-changed," said Messina. "They're not even at the table. Women are not considered as high risks, so they go out after release with no skills, often into the same environment that brought them into prison in the first place. Their needs are different, their wounds are different, their healing is different."

Unless they have family that is not part of the problem, or unless they can find a nonprofit reentry organization with available bandwidth, women approach the afterlife on their own.

A few years ago the Texas-based Prison Entrepreneurship Program, which has helped many men into post-prison careers, launched two small pilot programs for, as CEO Bryan

118　Kelley puts it, "the ladies." Texas incarcerates more women, in raw numbers, than any other state. (PEP, in fact, was founded in 2004 by a woman, Catherine Hoke, who resigned in 2009 after admitting to sexual affairs with formerly incarcerated students.) The women in the pilot programs often outperformed the men in entrepreneurial aptitude, Kelley told me. They came up with more realistic business plans, and were better at multitasking. But things didn't click. For one thing, reentry was more scattered. "Men typically go where the work is, and the ladies typically go where their kids are," Kelley said. "They dispersed all over the state and we didn't really find a critical mass in any one city" where PEP could concentrate the support needed for a happy landing.

Also, he said, women's psychological pain runs deeper, or at least they wear the trauma more openly. Kelley recalled doing a round of speed dating–style interviews with a half dozen women in the pilot program, asking about their backgrounds and business aspirations. Four of them broke down in tears talking about their path to prison. PEP ended up spinning off the women's program.

Stephanie Covington was designing addiction treatment programs for the exclusive Betty Ford Center in the late 1980s when she met a warden who invited her to spend a couple of days with women on the opposite end of privilege. She went on to create the California-based Center for Gender and Justice, advising prisons in the United States and abroad on how to cope with trauma.

Covington says some women's prisons get some things right but she has yet to find one she would offer as a model. I asked about her work at Las Colinas Detention and Reentry

Facility, a county jail near San Diego, which was built from scratch to be a showplace of progressive incarceration. Although jails are generally for people awaiting trial or serving short sentences, California, under a US Supreme Court order to reduce its severe prison overcrowding, has transferred thousands of prisoners to serve their remaining years in jails, which are not normally designed for long-term stays. Covington was a consultant on Las Colinas, which was planned with ample space for enrichment programs, lawns lined with palm trees, a coffee station, volleyball courts, and other recreational facilities. The jail has won praise as a gold standard in corrections, but Covington withholds her applause. She describes Las Colinas as something of a Potemkin village, a great facility short on programming content, governed by petty rules, and lacking in planning for reentry. The landscaped campus is off-limits to women in restrictive housing. "You have this big beautiful yard and probably a third of the women aren't allowed to leave their housing units and use the yard," she said.

Formerly incarcerated women say at least as demoralizing as the fear of physical violence are the constant low-grade humiliations and head games, intended to keep prisoners off-balance. Jennifer Toon said when women bled through the flimsy prison-issued sanitary pads, some COs would refuse a replacement until the prisoners' uniforms were badly bloodied, then post their names on a "wall of shame."

Morgan Godvin recalls one movie night when three hundred women lined up at the main entrance to the prison rec center, where there were never enough chairs. A CO eyed the orderly queue, then very deliberately opened a side door instead, setting off a stampede.

For women in prison, one prized relic of normalcy is makeup, restricted in most prisons, in part because lipstick and mascara have been used to smuggle in LSD, Ecstasy, or other drugs.

"Contraband for us was makeup and perfume," said Toon. "Women would come back from visitation and they would chop up the makeup they got, put it in these little baggies, and sell them. There is something really dehumanizing about being incarcerated, and makeup just made the girls feel better about themselves."

In a piece called "Fakeup," Simone Weichselbaum reported for the Marshall Project on the ingenuity female prisoners employ to supplement the few cosmetics sold at the prison commissary.

> For hair gel, soak a Jolly Rancher in a cup of hot water, add a dab of body lotion, apply. . . . For eye shadow, break open a colored pencil, crush into a powder, mix into a clump of baby powder, dab on the eyelids. To make an eye pencil, sharpen a colored pencil on a concrete wall and apply the point delicately on the eyelids. For foundation, use as much coffee as needed to match one's complexion, pour the amount into a dollop of regular face cream, stir and enjoy. M&Ms serve multiple fakeup needs: Mix the sweet candy-coated shells with hot water to make a lip stain. Crush the leftover nut—if using peanut M&Ms—into a spoonful of face cream, creating a protein-packed facial mask.

The most obvious thing that sets women apart: they have babies. A Johns Hopkins study of pregnancy in prison found that in a one-year period, from 2016 to 2017, 753 women gave birth while incarcerated in federal or state prisons. Since twenty-eight states, including New York and California, declined to participate in the survey, the actual number is probably at least double that. For these new mothers, the experience can be devastating.

Although the federal prison system in 2018 outlawed the barbaric practice of shackling mothers during childbirth, twenty-three states have no such restriction, so the experience of labor can be excruciating. "Women subjected to restraint during childbirth report severe mental distress, depression, anguish, and trauma," according to a 2017 report from the American Psychological Association.

Shackled or not, women face more profound distress after labor. In most prisons, mothers surrender their babies to relatives or foster care within a few days of birth. Only eight states—Illinois, Indiana, Nebraska, New York, Ohio, South Dakota, Washington, and West Virginia—have nursery units where prisoners can stay with their babies, in most cases at least until their first birthday, forging the attachment essential to a baby's emotional development.

The oldest and most intensively studied nursery ward is at the women's maximum-security Bedford Hills Correctional Facility, in affluent Westchester County, New York. Begun in the early 1900s as a reformatory for "delinquent and wayward girls," Bedford Hills had a reputation for being more paternalistic than punitive. In the 1980s—under the leadership of a progressive warden named Elaine Lord and a charismatic nun named Sister Elaine Roulet—the prison created a children's center with a playroom where mothers could spend visits with their kids and get parenting advice.

122   "Eighty-five percent of the women who come to New Bedford are mothers," said Judith Clark, who spent most of her
thirty-seven prison years at Bedford Hills and helped start the
children's center and nursery there. "We built the children's
center as a place you could come for help, and then get absorbed
into that community." Clark was part of a group of radicals who
robbed a Brinks armored car in 1981, killing a security guard and
two police officers. She became a model of rehabilitation, won
parole in 2019, and still works with women reentering the world
after prison. While incarcerated, she wrote a master's thesis on
the impact of a prison environment on the relationship between
women and their children.

New Clark worries about the replacement of in-person
contact with "tele-visits," which are cheaper and more conve-
nient for administrators but less intimate.

The nursery at Bedford Hills draws pregnant women from
New York's three female prisons and from jails in most of the
state's sixty-two counties, screening out women with histories
of child abuse or crimes—such as arson—that could put children at risk. A nonprofit called Hour Children provides about
fifty women a year—before the COVID-19 pandemic outbreak
suspended most prison programming—with services including
doulas, lactation consultants, parenting classes, access to a
pediatrician, and supervised day care while the mothers attend
school or therapy. The new mothers also get case managers to
plan their return to society.

Jane Silfen, the project director, estimates the state pays
about $250,000 a year, supplemented by a grant of $50,000 for
doulas and lactation specialists. Donors provide baby clothes
and toys—so generously that Bedford shares this treasure with

parents in other prisons who can't afford Christmas gifts for their children.

The payoff is tangible. Mary W. Byrne of the Columbia University Medical Center has studied the short-term and long-term effects of the Bedford Hills program and concluded that the babies bonded successfully and developed normally, and the mothers—many of whom had traumatic childhoods themselves—found purpose and direction. Only 10 percent of the women she tracked were sent back for parole infractions, and only 4 percent for new crimes—a fraction of the return rates for women in the general prison population.

Another study by Byrne, Barbara Blanchard-Lewis, and Lorie S. Goshin in 2014 examined the outcomes for children who spent their first months in a US prison nursery. Behavioral development in forty-seven preschool children who lived in a prison nursery was compared with sixty-four children from a large national dataset who were separated from their mothers because of incarceration. "Separation was associated with significantly worse anxious/depressed scores, even after controlling for risks in the caregiving environment. Findings suggest that prison nursery co-residence with developmental support confers some resilience in children who experience early maternal incarceration."

Stephanie Covington says that in her years working with women's prisons she has encountered several excuses for the scarcity of nurseries, which she itemized in a terse email:

1. fear . . . liability for children
2. money . . . we can't afford to do this

3. ignorance . . . if the women cared about their children they wouldn't "do drugs" or "commit a crime"

4. punitive . . . "this decreases motivation to get out"

The idea that separating women from their newborns is cruel to both has waxed and waned in this country's corrections practice. It was more widely accepted in the 1940s, when thirteen states had laws allowing incarcerated mothers to keep their children in prison with them. By the 1970s, many of those laws had been repealed, with policymakers citing security and liability, potential harm to child development, plus the trauma of eventual separation for children of women serving long sentences. By the 1980s, prison nursery units were widely held to be the best answer, but they were deemed too costly and cumbersome.

As in so many aspects of criminal justice, America is an outlier. The most recent data I could find, a 1987 survey by the Alliance of Non-Governmental Organizations on Crime Prevention and Criminal Justice, found that, of seventy nations queried, "only Suriname, Liberia, the Bahamas, and the US routinely separated imprisoned mothers from their infants."

The Other Prisoners

Most prisons seem designed as much to deflate the spirit as to confine the body. With their grey walls, clanging doors, artificial light and stale air, they are gloomy places quite apart from their mission as prisons. Ever-present rats, roaches, slime, and excrement make institutions like Walpole all the more inhospitable. People do not cheerfully go to work in such places.
—*Prison Officers and Their World*, 1988

"Officer after officer will tell you: There's no way in hell you'd want your kid to be a CO." ... It was "a life sentence in eight-hour shifts."
—*Newjack: Guarding Sing Sing*, 2000

It is getting in my blood. The boundary between pleasure and anger is blurring. To shout makes me feel alive. I take pleasure in saying no to prisoners. ... Who am I becoming?
—*American Prison*, 2018

Brian Dawe says that in his forty years in corrections he has never met a frontline prison officer who wakes up in the morning thinking, "I can't wait to get to work today." Dawe can point to statistics that roughly quantify the toll of the job: a rate of PTSD higher than that of soldiers returning from Iraq, a suicide rate at least seven times that of civilians, plus divorce and substance abuse levels "through the ceiling."

It is work that does not command a great deal of respect. In popular culture, Dawe notes, prison officers are portrayed as "a bunch of knuckle-draggers, maybe a hair better than the inmates and in most cases not even there."

Dawe started work as a CO in 1982 in Massachusetts because he had a kid on the way and prison work was paying better than flipping burgers. He came up through the union ranks and is now national director of One Voice United, which serves as an advocate and intelligence network for more than fifty unions representing prison workers. As Dawe likes to point out, "We hold the keys to change, because without us there won't be any."

Indeed, almost every even modestly successful reform attempt I've encountered depends on at least the grudging acquiescence, if not the active cooperation, of the men and women who work there.

But COs are widely regarded, on the left, as sadists in uniform; on the right, as soft targets for budget-cutters. Prison reformers view the officers—and in particular their unions— as incorrigible defenders of an inhumane status quo. Philanthropies and universities that work with the incarcerated often regard prison officers as an afterthought, or an obstacle, if they regard them at all.

When the coronavirus hit San Quentin, Jody Lewen's college-in-prison team easily found donors to buy gift bags of soap, energy bars, and other treats for thousands of prisoners. The team also—"for humanitarian and strategic reasons"—arranged for food trucks to pull up between shifts and serve free meals to the prison staff. Some donors balked at chipping in for that gesture of sympathy for workers who had been thrust into the role of first responders.

"It's amazing how many people are attracted to the prisoners but have nothing but contempt for the people working there," Lewen said.

The image of officers as thugs is not without foundation, of course. The Marshall Project has written extensively about prison brutality, including Tom Robbins's 2015 account of a horrific beating in Attica that prompted a Justice Department investigation, accelerated the installation of cameras inside the prison, and was a Pulitzer finalist.

There is also a subtler, pervasive form of control that some prison wag long ago dubbed "The Zo"—for The Twilight Zone. A precocious Yale student named Patrick Doolittle dug into a huge archive of prison writing, and for his senior thesis identified three stages of this low-grade psychological warfare. First, guards mess with the prisoners' heads using deliberately disorienting rules and impossible tasks. The prisoners try to keep their grip on reality by clinging to details—days until parole, prices of items in the commissary, the minutiae of routine. But the guards escalate, inflicting arbitrary transfers or random stints in isolation. (We turned Doolittle's ninety-six-page thesis into a prize-winning animated video, illustrated by Molly Crabapple and narrated by Michael K. Williams.)

128   Prison officers in turn sometimes complain about "free college for criminals" and other benefits not as readily available to the corrections staff. Some college-in-prison programs have tried to win over prison staff by including them. A 2019 survey conducted by the Alliance for Higher Education in Prison found that about a fifth of college-in-prison programs offered some services to corrections staff, including scholarships, professional development courses, lecture series, or "advising." St. Louis University, a private Jesuit school, runs separate associate degree courses for prison staff at a state maximum-security prison in Bonne Terre, an hour's drive south of the St. Louis campus. "Providing the same opportunity for the staff is something that helps make things happen for our incarcerated students," said Julie O'Heir, the program manager. But chronic understaffing makes for unpredictable work schedules. Staff enrollment in the university's classes on a typical day is about twenty employees out of eight hundred, and most of those are clerical and administrative staff rather than COs.

More often, notions of including staff have been stymied by cost and a lack of interest from correctional officers. Max Kenner of the Bard Prison Initiative says treating prisoners and officers as peers violates the hierarchical order. "Once you have inmates and staff in the same classroom, it ceases to be a prison."

Kenner recalled that Bard sought to alleviate staff resentment by creating scholarships for children of COs, but the plan was vetoed by New York State on grounds that "it would be perceived as a bribe."

In many states, prisons are so thinly staffed that they can barely do the job of containment, let alone cultivate the relationships with residents that facilitate rehabilitation in progressive

European prisons. If you divide the American prison population
by the number of correctional officers, you get a staffing ratio of
roughly five prisoners per CO, which sounds manageable. But
the prisoners are there all day, every day, while the staff works
eight-hour shifts. So on a given shift each officer is in charge of
about twenty prisoners.

These, of course, are very rough averages. In some facilities,
owing to budget cuts and high staff turnover, the ratio is much
higher. Dawe says that he has had more than sixty men in his
charge at one time.

Understaffing means overtime, which puts even greater
strain on budgets and on an already weary, stressed-out work-
force. Some prisons resort to a practice called "augmentation,"
drafting cooks, nurses, and secretaries to fill in as guards when
trained COs aren't available. All of this makes for a tightly
wound environment.

In her 1988 Massachusetts study, *Prison Officers and Their
World*, Kelsey Kauffman disputes "the conventional wisdom
that men who go to work in prisons are predisposed to violence, or revel in authority, or have unusually punitive attitudes
toward lawbreakers. . . . Critics of prisons should not comfort
themselves with the idea that, forced into the same circumstances, they would behave more nobly—or more effectively—
than did the officers of the Massachusetts prison system. The
intractable problems posed by prisons are not rooted in the
identities or characters of officers or inmates. The problems are
much more fundamental. They are rooted in the nature of the
goals prisons are erected to serve."

When Kauffman titled her final chapter "Prisoners All," she
seemed to mean not just the prisoners and staff but the society

130   that walled itself off from the moral compromises required to sustain such a system.

Dawe insists there is strong support among frontline prison workers not just for hiring more of them and paying them better but for training them to be more than gatekeepers with truncheons.

"So much of our training is self-defense, and we need that, no question about that," he told me, "but the aspect we're not being trained on is intercommunication with the inmate population. We need better de-escalation training, we need emotional intelligence training, we need to train to deal with individuals as individuals. We're not trained in these social skills."

This is a relatively novel argument coming from COs, but it is not a new thought. Ted Conover, the journalist who spent a year undercover as a rookie guard in Sing Sing prison, cited a report prepared for the New York State Assembly by a select committee on prisons. It included an eloquent plea to the legislators to emphasize social skills in the recruiting and training of officers:

> It is not like a man's driving a herd of oxen or working a piece of machinery . . . it is controlling the minds of men, no two of which are alike—it is curbing their tempers, whose manifestations are infinitely various—it is directing their motives which are as diverse as their personal appearance or physical conformation. And it requires an intimate knowledge, if not of human nature at large, at least of the habits, tempers, and dispositions of the men immediately under their charge. . . . This consideration, so evidently the

dictate of good sense, seems to be entirely overlooked in
the government of our prisons.

The report was filed in 1851.

Oregon has a way of living up to the Fred Armisen and Carrie Brownstein TV spoof, *Portlandia*. The state prison system has a Wellness and Equity Administrator? Of course it does. The maximum-security penitentiary features a Japanese healing garden? Indeed. And, naturally, the state's correctional regimen is called, with perhaps a trace of self-satisfaction, "The Oregon Way."

Like North Dakota, Pennsylvania, and other states, Oregon studied Norway, but what set it apart from prison systems in most other states is that Oregon has declared the correctional staff—not the prisoners—to be their primary focus. The aim is to reduce stress and violence, improve their feelings of autonomy on the job, and ultimately change the culture. It is one of the country's most ambitious attempts to enlist the frontline staff as allies in rehabilitation.

"At its foundation," the mission statement proclaims, "the Oregon Way is about prioritizing employee health and well-being by normalizing the correctional environment and, in turn, improving the outcomes for incarcerated people," who in Oregon are referred to as AICs—adults in custody.

Oregon's wake-up call came during an eighteen-month period in 2012–2013 when four employees of the Oregon Department of Corrections killed themselves. A survey of corrections officers found one in three had symptoms of post-traumatic stress disorder, such as hypervigilance, distraction, and waking

132   nightmares. Brie Williams, a medical doctor and the executive director of Amend, a prison reform nonprofit that works with Oregon, says COs also suffer extraordinarily high rates of more bread-and-butter problems like diabetes, obesity, hypertension, and heart failure.

Williams came to the criminal justice system as an expert medical witness in cases where defendants were awaiting trial in solitary confinement. Gathering evidence of the mental damage caused by prolonged isolation, she began to see prisons as "an arm of the healthcare system."

"I had this moment when it hit me that we're all on the same side," Williams told me. "That US prisons had failed us—the people who live in them, the people who work in them, and their families and communities."

In its first response, the Oregon Department of Corrections carved out quiet staff spaces "conducive to de-stressing," organized family "wellness events," introduced healthy options for staff meals, and otherwise tried to cultivate a salubrious working environment. The corrections department joined forces with Amend, which is affiliated with the University of California, San Francisco, and began a series of trips to Norway, pointedly including not just the administration but rank-and-file COs.

It was a start, but a survey of staffers in early 2019 still found "ambivalent attitudes" toward their jobs. A typical officer reported having witnessed at least ten episodes of violence in the previous six months. Forty-seven percent said if they were offered a job doing something else for the same pay, they'd jump at the chance to leave.

The Oregonians stepped up their game, bringing in Norwegians to shadow the prison staff on the job, and reducing the

use of high-stress methods like solitary confinement and forc-
ible cell extractions. Another sampling of the staff at the end
of 2019 found a significant boost in morale, a sense that things
were headed in the right direction.

Toby Tooley, formerly a captain at the state penitentiary
and later a program manager at Amend, told me they have seen
a "drastic fall-off in assaults on staff" and a sharp decline in
sick leave. But prison officials prefer to describe the changes
anecdotally—the old-school CO patiently coaxing a prisoner
with dementia to eat his breakfast, the troubled soul who was
persuaded to stop smearing feces on his cell wall—or simply as
a new vibe.

"I don't know how dark it could have gotten, but I know that
I wasn't happy with the person I was becoming," Tooley said.
"I'm happy with the person I've become now."

Brandon Kelly, a twenty-three-year veteran of prison work who
became superintendent of the maximum-security Oregon State
Penitentiary, said, "When I was a corrections officer I hated
nothing more than somebody coming down telling me how to
do my job." Now COs are given more of a say in tailoring life on
the cell blocks.

"One of the things that's hard to articulate: when you walk
through the prison you kind of measure success by the way it
feels," Kelly told me. "Today it feels like a better place than it did
ten years ago or five years ago."

Aliza Kaplan, director of a criminal justice reform clinic
at Lewis and Clark University Law School in Portland, says the
Oregon Way has taken firmer hold in the populous Willamette
Valley, less so in the more remote prisons, where "you may have

134   to wait six months to get into an AA meeting." But at places like the state penitentiary in Salem, the staff-first approach has built a degree of trust, if not rapport, between staff and prisoners, including shared programming, Kaplan said. "At evening classes half the turnout is COs in their civvies."

Oh, and that healing garden? It was the brainstorm of the prison's Asian Pacific Family Club, which raised the money and enlisted a Japanese designer. It has thirty trees (trimmed low so as not to obstruct the view from the prison watchtowers), a rock garden, a koi pond, a waterfall, and a wooden bridge. Staff and prisoners did the landscaping and, together, they tend to the pruning and watering.

"It's one of the most incredible spaces you could ever imagine in a prison," Kaplan said.

Sing Sing

Five years and many stories after my breakfast with Neil Barsky, I stepped down as editor of the Marshall Project. To keep a hand in the world of criminal justice, I volunteered to teach a weekly journalism seminar inside the Sing Sing Correctional Facility, up the Hudson River from New York City.

Sing Sing was built in the 1820s with no illusions about penitence or redemption. Prisoners did the construction, using marble they hacked from a nearby quarry. Alexis de Tocqueville and his friend Gustave de Beaumont made it the first stop on their tour of American prisons in 1831, and reported that the regimen was hard labor enforced by frequent application of the whip. It was the antithesis of the idealistic novelty the French visitors would encounter later at Eastern State Penitentiary.

Because it's only an hour by train from Manhattan, and because it has had modern wardens who understand the dangers of idle hands, Sing Sing today has a relative abundance of programs, including college courses run by Hudson Link for Higher Education in Prison (my point of entry), the Bard

136   Prison Initiative, Rehabilitation Through the Arts, and others.
A museum, under construction in a former power house just
outside the prison perimeter, promises to commemorate "the
history of punishment in America and the creation and development of the penitentiary system and associated reform
movements in America."

There are no whips, but prison is still fundamentally about
control, and the system takes great pains to impress that on
visitors.

Order, as in most American prisons, is built on a foundation of mistrust. Volunteers undergo a few hours of orientation, the main purpose of which is to instruct us in the ways
prisoners cannot be trusted. The docudrama miniseries *Escape
at Dannemora*—based on the true story of two prisoners who
tunneled out of a New York prison—is presented as the ultimate case study in how incarcerated men befriend, seduce, and
blackmail to get favors, to get contraband, and—in the case of
"Dannemora"—to get out.

Prison officers seem to see visiting volunteers as especially
easy marks for manipulative prisoners. So there is an emphasis
on "boundaries"—not just physical but emotional. The volunteer information packet goes beyond the dress code and the ban
on cell phones to instruct us that we must maintain a professional distance. We are never to divulge personal information
about ourselves. Volunteers may not correspond with or accept
phone calls from any inmate in the state system. "Care should
be taken to avoid becoming emotionally involved with inmates,"
we are warned. It is strongly recommended that students and
teachers not be on a first-name basis.

To bend the rules, even those that might strike an outsider
as arbitrary, is to set foot on the slippery slope to chaos. On the
Thursday afternoon in February when I arrived at the gate for
my first class, my entry was delayed half an hour because my
volunteer ID identified me as "Bill" while my driver's license
said "William." This discrepancy would delay my admission at
every subsequent visit, and seemed to amuse the staff. Each
week I was eventually issued a temporary pass and allowed to
board the van that delivers volunteers across the razor-wired
campus to the prison school.

All of this caution is probably prudent—Sing Sing has its
share of violence, drugs, and gangs, and volunteers are not corrections officers—but it pretty quickly dashes any notion that
such a prison might adopt the ethos of progressive European
prisons, where rehabilitation (and safety) depend on a healthy,
observant rapport. It is hard to imagine anything so normal
taking root in a Sing Sing cell block.

Sixteen men signed up for my seminar, "Introduction to
News," an overview of American journalism and its discontents.

I knew almost all of my students were serving sentences
that ended with the phrase ". . . to life," which usually means
someone died. Most were Black or brown, in their late forties
and fifties. All sixteen of them were "alumni," meaning they had
already earned at least one college degree while doing their time.
So, not without aspirations.

The mantra of rehabilitation is that no one should be permanently defined by the worst thing they've done. I've seen enough
men and women grasp second chances (or third, or fourth) that
I've become a believer in the possibility of redemption. But for

many, probably most, of the people who end up in prison, their crime was more than a random event. It had roots and a context.

My first homework assignment at Sing Sing was one I'd given to undergraduates at Princeton, where I had taught a writing seminar the previous semester: Describe a scene, something you have witnessed, in a few hundred words. Use details and dialogue to show me what you saw, to take me there. The resulting essays were unlike anything my Princeton undergrads turned in. Two of the scenes involved children discovering dead bodies. One described a teenage visit to a brothel. Two recounted the ritual humiliation of a prison strip search. No one described a birthday party or a camping trip. There seemed to be no parents in the vignettes. Only one related a happy experience—discovering a favorite video game in the prison building reserved for family visits.

By the fourth week I could connect most of the faces with names and some of the names with personalities—just in time for COVID-19 to shut the gates of New York State prisons to outsiders. In prisons and jails, the virus ran wild. Physical distancing is not easy in a place of bunk beds, chow lines, and communal showers; hand sanitizer (containing alcohol) is contraband; testing and vaccinating prison inmates—or, for that matter, staff—was not an urgent priority at first.

Even relatively progressive corrections systems fell abysmally short. Juan Moreno Haines, a prisoner who works as an editor at the *San Quentin News* in California, has written extensively about how overcrowding and ineptitude contributed to the toll of the virus. At one point officials gathered 120 inmates from another facility, some showing symptoms of infection, and bused them *into* San Quentin, without testing. Twenty-eight

prisoners and a correctional sergeant died of COVID-19 in what
a judge called "the worst epidemiological disaster in the history
of California corrections." The court called the failure to pro-
tect prisoners and staff "morally indefensible and constitution-
ally untenable."

Sing Sing fared better, though inmates reported the
response was haphazard at best. As of Christmas 2021, the
prison had confirmed five prisoners dead from the virus and
scores more infected.

As the year ended, I connected with two of my Sing Sing students who had been paroled in July. Mark Dixon and Wilfredo
Laracuente both went away in their twenties and returned to
the free world middle-aged. Both were convicted of murders
fueled by drugs. Both had childhood opportunities but gave in
to the lure of the street. Both earned multiple college degrees
behind bars and both ended up playing mentors or life coaches
for other men.

Wilfredo Laracuente grew up in the Bronx, went to paro-
chial school, and even started college before he succumbed to
the gangster life. He put two bullets into a rival drug dealer.
About halfway through his twenty-year sentence, he was transferred to Sing Sing where he connected with the Osborne Association and became what in YouTube parlance would be called
an influencer. He is now the program coordinator for the Prison
Education Project at Columbia's Center for Justice.

He refers to himself as "habilitated." "The 're' in front means
it happened before. It never happened to me before."

Mark Dixon was a child of middle-class Buffalo—the lone
Black student on high school ski trips and hockey teams. He

140   traveled to Vienna with a music-school choir. (When he is asked
how an actual choirboy ended up in Sing Sing, he answers "PCP."
The hallucinogenic drug "took me into a world where I was the
uber-male.") While in Sing Sing he joined every program available, from the Jaycees to the prison debate team. He earned a
BA in behavioral science and a master of professional studies
degree from the New York Theological Seminary.

"After you go through your first Intro to Psychology course,
you begin to assess your own life," he told me. That led him to
confront the tightly held memory that he had been sexually
abused as a child. "In those classes you begin to correlate what
you've gone through with what other guys have gone through—
guys that you know, not just people you've heard on TV."

In February 2020, he was a speaker at a TEDx event at the
prison, where he talked about getting past the shame of child
sexual abuse. A few weeks later, he woke up feeling lethargic and
with no sense of smell, relatively mild symptoms of COVID-19.

Dixon, who was fifty-three when he was released, described
his reentry to the free world as "a soft landing," helped, per-
versely, by the pandemic, which left employers desperate for
healthy workers. (He took an assembly-line job with a man-
ufacturer of plastic components.) But he has not escaped the
collateral consequences of his record. He applied to move in
with his wife in Bay Shore, a hamlet outside of New York, but
she lives in subsidized Section 8 housing, off limits to individuals convicted of a serious felony. Instead, he was paroled
to his eighty-three-year-old mother's house, four hundred
miles northwest in Buffalo, where despite his impressive prison
resume he feels as though he's treated like the headstrong young
man he was when he was arrested.

A few months after his release, he opened his laptop and a notice popped up that "Your IP address has been compromised." To a man who had spent the last quarter century offline, this seemed to be a credible warning from the gods of Microsoft. He clicked and followed the instructions to the inevitable welcome-to-freedom moment: $1,500 of his savings from prison jobs siphoned away.

Dixon took it as a sign that his education in the outside world is just beginning. "That was my tuition."

Anyone who has taught in prison, even briefly, will tell you the experience is gratifying. "You sense it when you walk in the room," says Vivian Nixon, who has been both a student and a teacher behind bars. "These are thirsty, hungry students. They actually do the reading. And if they have access, they'll look up the footnotes, too."

Gratifying . . . and also disheartening, owing to the waste of human potential these students embody, and the inadequacy of our response. Many prison reformers and volunteers suffer bouts of fatalism and inadequacy. Even the best of them—some of whom I've introduced in this book—say they sometimes feel as if they are merely making a toxic system more palatable.

Nevertheless, they do it. Danielle Sered, the restorative justice advocate, likens them to pacifists who drive ambulances in war zones; they are no less anti-war.

Reformers measure success in human increments: Released prisoners who have a fighting chance because they learned to control their temper, or earned a college degree, or, thanks to liberal visitation policies, held their families together. Addicted and mentally ill offenders offered treatment in place of jail time.

142 Corrections officials who see their job as more than policing a warehouse of defective creatures. Policymakers who think of the imprisoned as constituents, not as props for fearmongering.

"When you ask somebody whose life is now working, what made the difference for them," said Elizabeth Gaynes of the Osborne Association, "they're not going to say a program. They're going to say a person. It'll be their drug counselor or their parenting teacher or their college professor. For all of them it comes down to: somebody made them see another possibility for themselves."

Despite disappointments and frustrations, these people make a small difference in the inhumanity of the system by making a big difference in the lives of individual human beings. This book is dedicated to them.

Many people have shared their time and expertise to further my continuing education in the criminal justice system. Most of them are cited in the text or endnotes, but some deserve special thanks.

I'm especially indebted to the late Stanford Law School criminologist Joan Petersilia, whose wisdom and common sense (she liked to describe herself as "liberal but not stupid") are missed by a legion of students, including this unregistered one.

Others teachers who have been especially helpful include Bruce Western at Columbia, Francis Cullen at University of Cincinnati, Jordan Hyatt at Drexel University, Jody Lewen of Mount Tamalpais College, and Kelsey Kauffman, each of whom read and gave me feedback on portions of my manuscript. Jeremy Travis has been a reliable source of thoughtful analysis as president of the John Jay College of Criminal Justice and then as a vice president for criminal justice at Arnold Ventures, an early benefactor of the Marshall Project.

For facilitating my own too-brief experience teaching in Sing Sing, I'm grateful to the Hudson Link for Higher Education in Prison, especially Sean Pica and Douglas Duncan.

For answering my questions about Europe's prisons, I thank Jan R. Strømnes, deputy warden at the Halden maximum security prison in Norway, and Susanne Gerlach, director of the prison system in Berlin.

Among the advocacy groups and think tanks that I've pestered over the years, the Vera Institute of Justice has been a treasury of research and analysis; thanks in particular to Nick Turner, Ryan Shanahan, and Mary Crowley. Likewise Adam

144   Gelb, first at Pew Research and more recently as a founder of the Council on Criminal Justice; Vivian Nixon of College and Community Fellowship; Brie Williams and Cyrus Ahalt at Amend; Soffiyah Elijah of the Correctional Association of New York and the Alliance of Families for Justice; Marc Mauer of the Sentencing Project; Liz Gaynes at the Osbourne Association; Barry Scheck and his colleagues at The Innocence Project; and Danielle Sered of Common Justice.

   Corrections departments are not always press-friendly, but several present and former top corrections officials described their attempts to apply the lessons of European prisons: in Connecticut, Scott Semple, Michael Lawlor, Angel Quiros, Sharonda Carlos, and Karen Martucci; in Pennsylvania, John Wetzel and the staff of SCI Chester; in North Dakota, Leanne Bertsch, Dave Krabbenhoft, Jeremy Holkup, and Daniel Lukach; in Oregon, Brandon Kelly, Heidi Steward, Kelly Raths, and Toby Tooley; in New Mexico, Gregg Marcantel; and in California, Jeanne Woodford.

   My colleagues at the Marshall Project provided much of the scaffolding on which this book was built. I leaned most heavily on the reporting of Maurice Chammah, Eli Hager, and Dana Goldstein. Marshall staffers who have been incarcerated—Lawrence Bartley, Donald Washington, and Keri Blakinger—checked my facts, told me stories, and connected me with other formerly or currently incarcerated sources. Managing editor Kirsten Danis, now at the *New York Times*, read a first draft and offered smart comments.

   Among the many other criminal justice journalists I admire, I'm especially grateful to Tom Robbins of the CUNY journalism school and Jennifer Gonnerman of the *New Yorker*, who took

me on my first visit to Sing Sing. I've benefited from a growing 145
cadre of journalists who found their calling behind bars—and
who remain there at this writing. In particular, I thank John J.
Lennon and Juan Moreno Haines.

Columbia Global Reports has discovered—or perhaps
invented—a sweet spot between long-form magazine journalism and the weighty tome, and enlisted editors who actually edit, which seems to be a rarity in today's publishing world.
My thanks to Nick Lemann, Jimmy So, Camille McDuffie,
fact-checker Sujay Kumar, copyeditor Leigh Grossman, and the
promotion team of Megan Posco and Allison Finkel.

And, of course, Emma Gilby Keller, my wisest critic, reliable
tech support, and the love of my life.

Prison has inspired a rich literature of scholarship, polemic, poetry, and journalism. The "Bookshelf" feature of the Marshall Project website curates some of the best.

For fresh voices from behind bars, in addition to the Marshall Project "Life Inside" essays, I recommend browsing the PEN America prison writing awards, the Prison Journalism Project's newsletter "Inside Story," the American Prison Writing Archive at Hamilton College, and the wonderful Ear Hustle podcast.

Below are a few books that helped shape my thinking.

For an understanding of how we got here:

THE NEW JIM CROW BY MICHELLE ALEXANDER

Still indispensable. Alexander's provocative 2010 bestseller is a skillfully argued takedown of the American criminal justice system. Ibram X. Kendi calls it "the spark that would eventually light the fire of Black Lives Matter." The 2020 edition includes Alexander's response to critics.

LOCKING UP OUR OWN: CRIME AND PUNISHMENT IN BLACK AMERICA BY JAMES FORMAN JR.

How is it possible that a system that so disproportionately punishes Black Americans won the support of so many Black leaders and communities? Forman adds important nuance to Alexander's indictment.

RACE TO INCARCERATE BY MARC MAUER

A decade before *The New Jim Crow* (as Michelle Alexander would be the first to attest), Marc Mauer, executive director of The Sentencing Project, tracked the explosive growth, the social and economic toll, and the futility of America's approach to punishment. Mauer later teamed up with the illustrator Sabrina Jones to produce a graphic-novel version.

PUNISHMENT AND INEQUALITY IN AMERICA AND HOMEWARD: LIFE IN THE YEAR AFTER PRISON BY BRUCE WESTERN

Western, an Australian-born sociologist now at Columbia University, published the research-rich and revelatory *Punishment and Inequality,* back in 2006, but it holds up well. He documents, among other discoveries, how the exclusion of prisoners from government statistics hides the true extent

of racial inequality, and how the experience of prison condemns unskilled
Black men to a lower caste in society. *Homeward* portrays a reentry system
built for failure.

For memoirs of the prison experience:

A QUESTION OF FREEDOM BY R. DWAYNE BETTS

Betts was sent away at age sixteen for a carjacking. He is now an award-
winning poet with a law degree from Yale, and he brings both his creative
and his analytical skills to the story of his eight years behind bars.

CORRECTIONS IN INK BY KERI BLAKINGER

Blakinger, who now reports for the Marshall Project, has written a worthy
successor to *Orange Is the New Black*—a harrowing memoir of her descent
from white privilege to anorexia to heroin to incarceration.

For reporting on the toxic culture of prison:

BLOOD IN THE WATER: THE ATTICA PRISON UPRISING OF 1971 AND ITS LEGACY BY HEATHER ANN THOMPSON

Thompson makes clear in her scrupulous account of the nation's bloodiest
prison uprising that the riots, often portrayed as a rampage of leftist radicals, were fueled by the quotidian humiliations of prison life.

NEWJACK: GUARDING SING SING BY TED CONOVER

Conover's account of his year as a rookie correctional officer at the Sing Sing
maximum security prison is—besides being an astonishing feat of underground journalism—a convincing demonstration that our prison system
brutalizes everyone it touches.

AMERICAN PRISON BY SHANE BAUER

Inspired by Conover, Bauer signed up as an entry-level guard at a prison in
Louisiana. He chose a prison run by the giant private Corrections Corporation of America, and the book weaves together a grotesque portrait of incarceration today with a history of for-profit captivity dating back to the slave
plantations.

148   *PRISON OFFICERS AND THEIR WORLD* BY KELSEY KAUFFMAN

Kauffman's 1988 study of Massachusetts prisons was ahead of its time. It is out of print, but available in some libraries.

For those interested in going deeper into the social science research, here are two anthologies:

CRIME AND PUBLIC POLICY EDITED BY JAMES Q. WILSON AND JOAN PETERSILIA

This rich sample of criminal-justice scholarship is fair-minded and written for lay readers as well as academics.

REINVENTING AMERICAN CRIMINAL JUSTICE EDITED BY MICHAEL TONRY AND DANIEL S. NAGIN

More prescriptive than *Crime and Public Policy*, it musters science on behalf of reforming every aspect of criminal justice, from policing to parole.

For a sense of how they do prison elsewhere:

INCARCERATION NATIONS BY BAZ DREISINGER

Dreisinger, an English professor at the John Jay College of Criminal Justice, visits prisons in nine countries, from Rwanda to Norway. She finds in each prison a reflection of the society that built it, and lessons for our own. She is an observant and compassionate guide.

NOTES

INTRODUCTION

12 Neil Barsky: Barsky was a reporter for the *Wall Street Journal*, where his work frequently got under the skin of a real estate mogul named Donald J. Trump. ("Of all the writers who have written about me, probably none has been more vicious than Neil Barsky of The Wall Street Journal," the future president declared in *Trump: The Art of the Comeback*. Neil had the comment framed.)

13 roughly twice that of Russia's and Iran's: World Prison Brief, a database maintained by the University of London, prisonstudies.org.

14 has been in a gradual but steady decline: Jacob Kang-Brown, Chase Montagnet, and Jasmine Heiss, "People in Jail and Prison in 2020," Vera Institute of Justice, January 2021.

14 thirty-four states, red and blue, simultaneously reduced incarceration and crime rates: "New Analysis: States Lowered Crime and Incarceration Rates Simultaneously," Brennan Center for Justice, June 8, 2016.

CHAPTER ONE

17 Eastern State Penitentiary: Online tour of the facility, now a museum, and timeline,

easternstate.org/research/history -eastern-state/timeline.

18 Charles Dickens, after a visit in 1842: Quoted in Chai Woodham, "Eastern State Penitentiary: A Prison with a Past," *Smithsonian Magazine*, September 30, 2008.

18 Tocqueville found the Philadelphia penitentiary regimen suffocating: *On the Penitentiary System in the United States and Its Application to France* (1833). Translated by Emily Katherine Ferkaluk (Springer International Publishing, 2018 edition).

19 from the tranquility of Buddhist meditation: Prison Outreach Program, Upaya Institute and Zen Center, 2021, upaya.org /social-action/prison-outreach.

19 to the blood sport of inmate rodeos in Louisiana: "Angola Prison Rodeo," Angola Museum at the Louisiana State Penitentiary, 2019.

19 "fashionable nowadays to say that only rehabilitation can justify confinement": Quoted in *Crime and Public Policy*, 2011, edited by James Q. Wilson and Joan Petersilia, p. 293.

19 "rehabilitation has been found to be ineffective": *Crime and Public Policy*, p. 293.

19 "punitive turn in American life": Michael S. Sherry, *The Punitive Turn in American Life: How the United States Learned to Fight*

150   *Crime Like a War* (The University of North Carolina Press, 2020).

19   **"stability of punishment":** Alfred Blumstein, interview, February 14, 2021, and "A Theory of the Stability of Punishment," in *Journal of Criminal Law and Criminology* 64, no. 2 (1973).

20   **had bipartisan support, albeit for contradictory reasons:** See, for example, Derek Neal and Armin Rick, "The Prison Boom and Sentencing Policy," *Journal of Legal Studies* 45, no. 1 (2016).

21   **conjured a myth of youthful "super-predators":** See Carroll Bogert and Lynnell Hancock, "Superpredators: The Media Myth That Demonized a Generation of Black Youth," the Marshall Project, November 20, 2020.

21   **set out to debunk rehabilitation:** Jerome G. Miller, "The Debate on Rehabilitating Criminals: Is It True That Nothing Works?" *Washington Post*, March 1989.

22   **who spent four months working undercover as a guard:** Shane Bauer, *American Prison: A Reporter's Undercover Journey into the Business of Punishment* (Penguin Press, 2018).

22   **some prison towns have become disenchanted:** Keri Blakinger, "Small Towns Used to See Prisons as a Boon. Now, Many Don't Want Them," the Marshall Project/NBC News, June 10, 2021.

23   **identified crime as the nation's most important problem:** Thirty-seven percent in 1994, cited by Peter Beinart in *The Atlantic*, May 1, 2013; 2 percent in 2012, Andrew Dugan, "Economy Still Top Problem in U.S. but Less So Than in Past," Gallup, December 20, 2012.

23   **a reform movement on the right:** Portions of this chapter were published by the *New Yorker* and the Marshall Project. They are updated and reprinted with permission.

27   **pointed to the previous great American exercise in decarceration:** Interview with Petersilia in 2015.

29   **studio at Yale run by the renowned architect Frank Gehry:** Bill Keller, "Reimagining Prison with Frank Gehry," *New Yorker*, December 21, 2017.

30   **Danielle Sered has pointed out:** "Is Prison the Answer to Violence?" the Marshall Project, February 16, 2017, and interview, May 5, 2021.

31   **joined an intensive two-year restorative justice course:** "Victim Offender Education Group (VOEG)," Insight Prison Project, n.d.

32   **to spend $5 billion for community violence–prevention measures:** John Schuppe, "Biden

Wants to Give Anti-violence
Groups $5 Billion. Here's How
It Could Be Spent," NBC News,
April 14, 2021.

32 **as Elizabeth Glazer, then
director of New York City's
criminal justice office:** Bill Keller,
"What Do Abolitionists Really
Want," the Marshall Project,
June 13, 2019.

33 **DeAnna Hoskins, president
of JustLeadershipUSA:** Bill Keller,
"What Do Abolitionists Really
Want."

33 **"I don't think that in my
lifetime we'll ever abolish
prisons":** Bill Keller, "What Do
Abolitionists Really Want."

34 **London Breed decrying
a "reign of criminals" in San
Francisco:** KQED, December 21,
2021, kqed.org/news/11899060
/vowing-to-end-reign-of
-criminals-destroying-our-city
-sf-mayor-breed-announces-latest
-tenderloin-crackdown.

34 **Eric Adams rethinking the
plan to close the Rikers Island
jail complex in New York:** *Politico*,
December 15, 2021.

34 **reminisced wistfully about
working with President Trump's
son-in-law, Jared Kushner:** Video
conference with board members of
the Marshall Project.

34 **By the waning days of
the Trump administration,**

even Pat Nolan: Pat Nolan,
"Beware of George Soros' Trojan
Horse Prosecutors," *American
Conservative*, September 11, 2020.

CHAPTER TWO

37 **the bedlam of Los Angeles
County's Twin Towers
Correctional Facility:** If you are
busted in LA and want to avoid the
county lockup you can pay to be
lodged in Beverly Hills, Seal Beach,
or other local jails. "Afraid of Jail?
Buy an Upgrade," Alysia Santos, the
Marshall Project, March 9, 2017.

38 **attempted to put a price on
the "social costs" of incarceration:**
"The Economic Burden of
Incarceration in the United States,"
2016.

38 **"worshipping the false
gods of randomized control
trials":** Jeremy Travis interview,
February 19, 2021.

39 **punishment assumes that
a crime was an act of free will:**
Francis T. Cullen and Cheryl
Lero Jonson, *Correctional Theory:
Context and Consequences,* second
edition (SAGE Publications, 2016);
interview with Francis Cullen,
March 26, 2001; and emails.

40 **should have eliminated crime
entirely by 1986:** Marc Mauer,
Race to Incarcerate (The New Press,
2006), p. 65.

40 **concluded that "selective
incapacitation":** William Spelman,

152   *Criminal Incapacitation* (Springer, 2010), pp. 311–312.

41   **followed two groups of men convicted of similar violent crimes:** David J. Harding et al, "A Natural Experiment Study of the Effects of Imprisonment on Violence in the Community," *Nature Human Behaviour* 3 (2019), pp. 671–677.

42   **A 2021 report in the journal *Crime and Justice*:** "Custodial Sanctions and Reoffending: A Meta-Analytic Review," vol. 50, no. 1, pp. 353–424.

42   **"some of those released from prison may be more likely to be involved in crime":** Bruce Western, *Punishment and Inequality in America* (Russell Sage Foundation, 2007), p. 187.

43   **68 percent of prisoners released from state prisons:** "5 Out of 6 State Prisoners Were Rearrested Within 9 Years of Their Release," US Department of Justice, Office of Justice Programs, May 23, 2018.

44   **45 percent of released prisoners were convicted of new crimes within three years:** Seena Fazel and Achim Wolf, "A Systematic Review of Criminal Recidivism Rates Worldwide: Current Difficulties and Recommendations for Best Practice," *PLoS ONE* 10, no. 6 (June 2015).

44   **concluded that nothing worked *reliably* or *predictably*:** Robert Martinson, "What Works? Questions and Answers About Prison Reform," the *Public Interest* (Spring, 1974). Reprinted in *National Affairs* 50 (Winter, 2022).

45   **"to have offenders learn a set of behavioral and cognitive skills":** Francis T. Cullen, *Correctional Theory*, p. 208.

45   **But with 95 percent of the prison population:** "Reentry Trends in the United States," US Department of Justice, Bureau of Justice Statistics, April 14, 2004.

CHAPTER THREE

50   **package of advice on how to orient prisons toward rehabilitation:** "Responsible Prison Project: Reshaping the Texas Prison System for Greater Public Safety," the Marshall Project, October 21, 2016.

51   **Flaherty expanded his manual:** Flaherty's book, published in May 2022, is called *Reshaping the Texas Prison System for Better Public Safety: An Inside View from a Texas Lifer.*

55   **"'Sir' to a convict:** Victor Hugo, *Les Miserables*, "Monsieur to a convict is a glass of water to a man dying of thirst at sea. Ignominy thirsts for respect." Translated by MacAfee and Fahnstock (Penguin, 1987), p. 76.

154   of Seclusion," *Bismarck Tribune*,
June 4, 2016.

71 **"We started to hire people
who wanted to be agents of
change":** Leann Bertsch, interview,
May 6, 2021, and follow-up emails.

73 **about half of them had been
won over to the new approach:**
Nathan Erickson, interview, June 2,
2021.

73 **"I remember feeling unsafe":**
Daniel Lukach, interview, May 17,
2021.

74 **prison's job as "making better
neighbors":** Dave Krabbenhoft,
interview, May 19, 2021.

CHAPTER SIX

75 **from stops by police:** Magnus
Lofstrom, Joseph Hayes, Brandon
Martin, and Deepak Premkumar,
"Racial Disparities in Law
Enforcement Stops," Public Policy
Institute of California, October
2021.

75 **acquiescence or outright
encouragement of corrections
officials:** Joseph Neff and Alysia
Santo, "Mississippi Prison Killings:
Five Factors Behind the Deadly
Violence," the Marshall Project,
January 8, 2020.

75 **"race is central to the social
order of prison":** Pyrooz interview,
November 16, 2021.

    Also, David Pyrooz and Scott
H. Decker, "We Spoke to Hundreds

of Prison Gang Members—Here's
What They Said About Life Behind
Bars," *The Conversation*, April 3,
2020.

77 **"who have never known
a Black person who wasn't a
convicted felon":** Elizabeth
Gaynes, interview, May 6, 2021, and
emails.

77 **gangs often offer criminal
opportunities on the outside:**
"Prison Gangs," US Department of
Justice, April 29, 2021, justice.gov
/criminal-ocgs/gallery/prison
-gangs.

77 **Black men are significantly
more likely to return to prison:**
"Black Men Have Higher Rates
of Recidivism Despite Lower
Risk Factors: Study," PhysOrg,
October 23, 2018.

78 **cannot be explained as
simply a society defending itself:**
Michelle Alexander, *The New Jim
Crow: Mass Incarceration in the Age
of Colorblindness* (The New Press,
2012) and a 2017 email exchange.

79 **"moral poverty":** See William
J. Bennett, John J. DiIulio Jr., and
John P. Walters, *Body Count: Moral
Poverty . . . and How to Win America's
War Against Crime and Drugs*
(Simon & Schuster, 1996).

80 **"The motivation for mass
incarceration was crime and
increased punitiveness":** Justin
Pickett, interview, April 6, 2021.

81   "How could it be that even after forty years of tough-on-crime": James Forman Jr., *Locking Up Our Own: Crime and Punishment in Black America* (Farrar, Straus and Giroux, 2017).

83   "Mass incarceration flows along the lines of social and economic inequality": Bruce Western, *Punishment and Inequality in America.*

83   **John Pfaff:** Bill Keller and Eli Hager, "Everything You Think You Know About Mass Incarceration Is Wrong," the Marshall Project, February 9, 2017.

86   "But these efforts were largely framed in race-neutral and therefore history-neutral terms": "Out from the Holocaust," the Marshall Project, December 20, 2018.

86   **lynching sites:** The National Museum for Peace and Justice in Montgomery tells the American story of racial terror.

86   **"1619 Project":** Nikole Hannah-Jones et al, *New York Times.*

CHAPTER SEVEN

87   **After the 1994 crime bill:** Gerard Robinson and Elizabeth English, "The Second Chance Pell Pilot Program: A Historical Overview," the American Enterprise Institute, September 2017.

87   **San Quentin, California's oldest state prison:** Bill Keller and Neil Barsky, "San Quentin Puts on a Happy Face," the Marshall Project, January 27, 2016.

88   **prisoners who take part in educational programming:** Robert Bozick, Jennifer L. Steele, Lois M. Davis, and Susan Turner, "Does Providing Inmates with Education Improve Postrelease Outcomes?" *Journal of Experimental Criminology* (May 2018).

89   **favors other ways to measure the impact of in-prison higher education:** Jody Lewen, multiple interviews and remarks at the 2017 commencement of the Berkeley Rhetoric Department.

91   "but we are up against a bigotry of expectations": Max Kenner, interviews, June 3 and July 8, 2021.

93   "The headhunters were much more educational than Yale": Kelsey Kauffman, "Academia in Prison: The Role of the University in an Era of Mass Incarceration," *Perspectives on History, The Newsmagazine of the American Historical Association*, February 1, 2015, and multiple interviews.

94   **exposing a network of white supremacists, called the Brotherhood:** Josephine Bode, a journalism graduate student at Ball State University in Muncie, recounted Kauffman's exploits in a

156   master's thesis that reads like the pitch for a TV thriller. "Challenging the Brotherhood" exists only as a hard copy in the Ball State library.

94   **"The class of about a dozen women studied civic literacy":** Eli Hager, 'Building Towards a Future," the Marshall Project, November 11, 2017.

CHAPTER EIGHT

97   **"welcome-to-freedom moments":** Bryan Kelley, interviews, July 14 and July 18, 2021.

98   **"mass incarceration has an afterlife":** Reuben Jonathan Miller, *Halfway Home: Race, Punishment, and the Afterlife of Mass Incarceration* (Little, Brown, 2021), p. 8.

99   **"if we furloughed all of my parole officers in New York State for three months":** Martin Horn, quoted in Bill Keller, "What Do Abolitionists Really Want," the Marshall Project, June 13, 2019.

99   **has suggested simply outsourcing supervision to nongovernmental organizations:** Vincent Schiraldi, quoted in Bill Keller, "What Do Abolitionists Really Want."

100   **first he was underground on the FBI's most wanted list:** Elizabeth Gaynes, interview, May 6, 2021, and emails.

101–102   **only 8 percent end up back in prison:** Outside reviewers were Baylor University and the Initiative for a Competitive Inner City, a nonprofit research organization.

102   **45,000 federal and state laws:** Reuben Jonathan Miller, *Halfway Home*, p. 9.

102   **Collateral Consequences Resource Center:** Interview with Margaret Love, June 24, 2021, and email follow-ups.

103   **Michelle Jones:** Eli Hager, "From Prison to Ph.D.: The Redemption and Rejection of Michelle Jones," the Marshall Project and the *New York Times*, September 13, 2017. Jones told friends the *Times* article was hurtful because (at my insistence) it began by naming her crime. She did not respond to my requests for an interview for this book.

107   **"Collateral consequences should be tailored to the crime, and limited":** Margaret Love, interview, June 26, 2021, and emails.

107   **"ban the box":** "Racial Profiling in Hiring: A Critique of New Ban-the-Box Studies," Collateral Consequences Resource Center, August 17, 2016.

108   **"right to be forgotten":** See *Martin v. Hearst*, US Court of Appeals for the Second District, decided January 28, 2015.

108 **Another eighteen countries have followed:** "Global Overview of Sex Offender Registration and Notification Systems," SMART, April 2014.

108 **belief that those who commit sex crimes are highly likely to be repeat offenders:** Adam Liptak, "Did the Supreme Court Base a Ruling on a Myth?" *New York Times*, March 6, 2017.

108–109 **found that most sex offenders do not commit new sex crimes:** Andrew J. R. Harris and R. Karl Hanson, "Sex Offender Recidivism: A Simple Question," Public Safety and Emergency Preparedness Canada, March 2004.

109 **registered sex offenders in Miami-Dade County, Florida:** Emily Kassie and Beth Schwartzapfel, "Banished," the Marshall Project, October 3, 2018.

CHAPTER NINE

111 **"The American prison system was built with men in mind":** Keri Blakinger, "Can We Build a Better Women's Prison," *Washington Post*, October 28, 2019.

112 **"what women tend to do is re-create family structures in prison":** Vivian Nixon, interview, March 24, 2021.

113 **"Everyone has a prison girlfriend":** Keri Blakinger, interview, August 4, 2021.

114 **"It was a very big deal on a woman's unit: 'I don't want to get moved'":** Jennifer Toon, interview, August 6, 2021.

114 **"They tell you it's a safety issue":** Stephanie Covington, interview, August 10, 2021.

114 **reporting of sexual violence has improved:** "PREA Data Collection Activities, 2021," US Department of Justice, Office of Justice Programs, June 2021.

115 **reported having been "sexually victimized":** Alan J. Beck and Candace Johnson, "Sexual Victimization Reported by Former State Prisoners, 2008," US Department of Justice, Office of Justice Programs, May 2012.

115 **is even more of a sexual horror show:** S. E. James, J. L. Herman, S. Rankin, M. Keisling, L. Mottet, and M. Anafi, "The Report of the 2015 U.S. Transgender Survey," National Center for Transgender Equality, 2016.

116 **"There was zero opportunity for college credit":** Morgan Godvin, interview.

116 **"But we won't talk about trauma":** Nena Messina, interview, August 20, 2021.

120 **ingenuity female prisoners employ to supplement the few cosmetics:** Simone Weichselbaum, "Fakeup," the Marshall Project, November 19, 2014.

158

120 **study of pregnancy in prison:** Carolyn Sufrin, Lauren Beal, Jennifer Clarke, Rachel Jones, and William D. Mosher, "Pregnancy Outcomes in US Prisons, 2016–2017," *American Journal of Public Health* 109, no. 5 (May, 2019), pp. 799–805.

121 **outlawed the barbaric practice of shackling mothers during childbirth:** Lori Teresa Yearwood, "Pregnant and Shackled: Why Inmates Are Still Giving Birth Cuffed and Bound," *The Guardian*, January 24, 2020.

121 **nursery units where prisoners can stay with their babies:** Hendrik DeBoer, "Prison Nursery Programs in Other States," OLR Research Report, March 30, 2012.

121 **oldest and most intensively studied nursery ward:** Interview with Jane Silfen, project manager for Hour Children, Aug 27, 2021.

122 **before the COVID-19 pandemic outbreak suspended most prison programming:** Caroline Lewis, "NY Women's Prison, Housing Mothers and Newborns, Hit by COVID-19 Outbreak," *Gothamist*, April 20, 2021.

123 **Mary W. Byrne:** "Mary Byrne Interview," Vera Institute of Justice, February 11, 2010.

123 **examined the outcomes for children who spent their first months in a US prison nursery:** Lorie S. Goshin, Mary W. Byrne, and Barbara Blanchard-Lewis, "Preschool Outcomes of Children Who Lived as Infants in a Prison Nursery," *Prison Journal* 94, no. 2 (June 2014), pp. 139–158.

124 **"only Suriname, Liberia, the Bahamas, and the US routinely separated imprisoned mothers from their infants":** Lorie Smith Goshin and Mary Woods Byrne, "Converging Streams of Opportunity for Prison Nursery Programs in the United States," *Journal of Offender Rehabilitation* 48, no. 4 (May 2009), pp. 271–295.

CHAPTER TEN

126 **who wakes up in the morning thinking:** Brian Dawe, interview June 14, 2021. Dawe and others also cite a widely circulated claim that life expectancy of correctional officers is fifty-nine years, compared to a national average of seventy-five years. This has been described by the fact-checkers at Politifact as "an urban legend."

126 **statistics that roughly quantify the toll of the job:** Caterina G. Spinaris, Michael D. Denhof, and Julie A. Kellaway, "Posttraumatic Stress Disorder in United States Corrections Professionals: Prevalence and Impact on Health and Functioning," US Department of Justice, Office

of Justice Programs, 2012; Lisa K. Richardson, B. Christopher Frueh, and Ronald Acierno, "Prevalence Estimates of Combat-Related PTSD: A Critical Review," *Australia and New Zealand Journal of Psychiatry* 44, no. 1 (January 2010), pp. 4–19.

127 **"for humanitarian and strategic reasons":** Jody Lewen, multiple interviews.

129 **you get a staffing ratio of roughly:** Here's the math: 2 million prisoners /400,000 officers = 5:1. Each officer works 5 of 21 shifts per week; so 5/21 or 24 percent of staff is on duty each shift—roughly 20.8 prisoners per officer.

130 **cited a report prepared for the New York State Assembly:** *Newjack*, Ted Conover.

131 **Oregon's wake-up call:** Cyrus Ahalt et al, "Transforming Prison Culture to Improve Correctional Staff Wellness and Outcomes for Adults in Custody 'The Oregon Way,'" *Advancing Corrections Journal* (2019).

132 **"I had this moment when it hit me that we're all on the same side":** Brie Williams, interview, March 10, 2021.

133 **"drastic fall-off in assaults on staff":** Toby M. Tooley, interview, July 16, 2021.

EPILOGUE

135 **Tocqueville:** *On the Penitentiary System in the United States and Its Application to France* (1833). Translated by Emily Katherine Ferkaluk (Springer International Publishing, 2018 edition).

136 **museum, under construction in a former power house:** "About the Project," Sing Sing Prison Museum.

136 ***Escape at Dannemora:*** The seven-episode series is on Showtime.

138 **bused them *into* San Quentin:** "We pleaded for social distancing here in San Quentin. The state refused and now COVID is raging," Juan Moreno Haines, *Los Angeles Times*, January 28, 2022.

139 **the response was haphazard at best:** John J. Lennon, "When Coronavirus Came to Sing Sing," *New York Magazine*, September 21, 2020.

Columbia Global Reports is a publishing imprint from Columbia University that commissions authors to produce works of original thinking and on-site reporting from all over the world, on a wide range of topics. Our books are short—novella-length, and readable in a few hours—but ambitious. They offer new ways of looking at and understanding the major issues of our time. Most readers are curious and busy. Our books are for them.

Subscribe to our newsletter, and learn more about Columbia Global Reports at globalreports.columbia.edu.